More
Put a Lid on It!

Small-Batch Preserving
Year Round

Macmillan Canada

Toronto

Canadian Cataloguing in Publication Data

Topp, Ellie, 1938–
    More put a lid on it!

Includes index.
ISBN 0-7715-7625-0
1. Canning and preserving. I. Howard, Margaret, 1930–. II. Title.

TX603.T66 1999   641.4   C99-930524-7

This book is available at special discounts for bulk purchases by
your group or organization for sales promotions, premiums,
fundraising and seminars. For details, contact: Macmillan Canada,
Special Sales Department, 29 Birch Avenue, Toronto, ON
M4V 1E2. Tel: 416-963-8830

Cover photo: Hal Roth
Cover design: Gord Robertson
Interior photos & illustrations courtesy of Bernardin Ltd.

Macmillan Canada
CDG Books Canada Inc.
Toronto, Ontario, Canada

1 2 3 4 5   KRO   03 02 01 00 99

We acknowledge the financial support of the Government of
Canada through the Book Publishing Industry Development
Program for our publishing activities.

Printed in Canada

Contents

Acknowledgements

The extensive consumer and media support given *Put a Lid on It!* encouraged Macmillan Canada and ourselves to produce a sequel. Creating *More Put a Lid on It!* has given the two of us the pleasure of continuing to work together in developing exciting new recipe ideas to share with our readers. Although geographically separated, the marvel of email has allowed us to work together as if living next door. We found ourselves exchanging electronic files almost daily. Thus we managed only two short working visits, but many long-distance telephone calls in between.

We continue to enjoy working with the talented staff at Macmillan Canada and are grateful for their support. Nicole de Montbrun, our editor, gave freely of her expertise, guidance and friendship in directing this book to completion. Copy editor Madeline Koch, page designer Gordon Robertson and photographer Hal Roth all provided their special skills. As always, our families provided critique and support. John Howard assisted in editing of the final manuscript and Clarke Topp provided expertise in evaluating the heating pattern of the flavoured oils.

We also wish to acknowledge the significant contributions made by the following: Foodland Ontario and Fatima Agostinho who gave us access to their files of fruits and vegetable recipes.

Tom Gleeson of the Health Protection Branch, Health Canada, and Dr. Pearl Peterkin, formerly of HPB, for their counsel on aspects of food safety.

Dr. Kamanzi and Ann Zebchuck of CFIA.

Judi Kingry, Marketing Manager, Bernardin Canada, Ltd., who reviewed the final manuscript and provided photographs and illustrations.

Marian Hebb who again worked out all the required legalities.

Marjorie Hollands and Katherine Younker for the analysis and approval of the Canadian Diabetes Association Food Choice Values for Light 'n' Low Sugar Spreads.

Dorothy Long, home economist for the Canola Oil Information Service in Saskatchewan, for her enthusiastic support of our treatment of flavoured oils.

Colleagues and friends who shared recipes with us: Raylene Nash of the Wild Blueberry Producers Association of Nova Scotia, Yvonne Tremblay, Toronto food consultant, Janet Jenkinson, London home economist, Lesley Cook, Jayne Rider, Fred Yule and Bob and Barbara Cline.

Introduction

OVERWHELMED by the interest in our first book, *Put a Lid on It!* and with many more preserving ideas we wished to share, we find ourselves putting "another lid" on a second book. The recipes in this edition are all new although the procedures we developed in the first book and the organization is the same as the first one. So those of you familiar with *Put a Lid on It!* will feel right at home. If you are new to preserving, however, don't worry: we'll take you carefully through the "ins and outs" of our simple approach.

Many of us remember our grandmothers spending long hours in the summer preserving the produce from their large gardens. While few of us have a desire to return to the era of preserving large quantities of food for the cold months, we are developing a taste for new flavours and want to use them to enhance an otherwise simple meal. We have discovered that a flavourful bit of chutney, a rich salsa, a crisp pickle, a special sauce, or a flavoured oil or vinegar adds much interest to your meals while fitting a healthy lifestyle. Jams, conserves, marmalades and jellies can be spread on toast, English muffins or tea biscuits with no added butter necessary. You won't miss it.

Preserving food is great fun and not at all difficult. When you decide to "put a lid on it," there are two important things you must do. The first is to destroy all microorganisms such as bacteria, moulds and yeasts naturally present in food to prevent them from spoiling the preserved product. Having done this, the second thing is to make sure your preserving containers are sealed in such a way that other organisms cannot enter. If these critters find their way "under the lid," they will cause your carefully prepared food to spoil.

1

Today's methods of preserving are much easier, thanks to innovations from jar manufacturers. The snap lids are much more foolproof than were the glass-topped sealer jars used in bygone days. And modern jars come in a variety of convenient sizes that let us preserve small amounts quickly without overwhelming our storage areas. The small batches featured in our book let you make a small amount of a tasty preserve in very short order.

We now have access to a wide variety of fruits and vegetables—some of which were unknown to North America until recently. Many of these fruits and vegetables, such as mangoes, papayas, fresh figs and even strawberries and a variety of peppers are now available year round. Almost all of our recipes can be made throughout the year with this greater availability. However, a few foods are only available for short times of the year. Seville oranges are a good example. They are usually in Canadian stores only in January and February. Other fruits and vegetables, although available throughout the year, may be of better quality at certain times. We believe the quality of our own locally grown produce is superior since it arrives fresh in our kitchens without extended storage. At other times, good imported produce is available—just remember, you may be paying more. So *Put a Lid on It!* again when the quality is finest and price is lowest.

Ways to Preserve Food

Heat, acid, sugar and freezing are the four ways to prevent food from spoiling when put under a lid.

1. By Heat

The easiest way to destroy microorganisms present in food is to heat the food. Processing is the word traditionally used when filled jars of food are heated to specific temperatures for specific lengths of time. The times and temperatures depend on the density of the food and the size of the jar.

All moulds, yeasts and most bacteria are destroyed at the temperature of boiling water. However, some bacteria, such as *Clostridium botulinum*, can form spores that withstand very high temperatures. Therefore, although this bacteria is destroyed by boiling-water temperatures, its spores may survive. These spores develop into bacteria that are able to grow in an airtight environment (such as a canning jar) and produce a poisonous toxin causing botulism. Fortunately these bacteria cannot grow in the presence of such acids as vinegar or lemon juice.

For preserving purposes, food can be divided into two categories—

High-Acid Foods and Low-Acid Foods

High-Acid Foods are sufficiently acidic to kill any spores that survive boiling-water processing. Most fruits, some vegetables and some tomatoes are high-acid foods. They can be processed at the lower temperatures reached with a boiling-water canner.

Low-Acid Foods are not sufficiently acidic to inhibit the growth of bacteria spores that can survive boiling-water temperatures. They must be preserved by processing in a pressure canner which reaches much higher temperatures than can be achieved with boiling-water methods. Pressure canning is used to process the canned foods we buy. In this book, we don't deal with pressure canning since few people have the equipment.

2. By Acid

Fortunately, low-acid foods can be safely preserved at boiling-water temperatures by adding acid. This is the secret of pickling. If the acid in a food is strong enough, most microorganisms cannot grow. Familiar acids used in this process are many types of vinegars and lemon juice. All our recipes have a pH value falling within the Agriculture Canada/Health Canada's definition of high acid foods. Thus, it is essential to measure the ingredients accurately and not alter either the amount of acid or the amount of vegetable. A few microorganisms are able to grow at high acid concentration. Therefore, it is now recommended that all pickled foods be processed in a boiling water canner for short periods of time.

3. By Sugar

Sugar present in high concentrations traps water in food, creating an environment where microorganisms cannot grow. Jams and jellies are preserved in this way. Moulds and some yeasts can grow on the surface of such foods, but only in the presence of air. An airtight seal achieved from heat processing prevents the growth of such moulds and yeasts.

4. By Freezing

Freezing stores food at such low temperatures that no microorganism growth can occur. However, some enzyme activity can still go on in vegetables, giving off flavours. To prevent this, vegetables are generally blanched briefly before freezing. Fruits may be frozen in their raw state. Several of our jams, spreads and curds are under a lid and frozen to extend their storage.

Easy Step-by-Step Preserving

1. Food Selection and Preparation

The *best* preserves result from using the *best* ingredients. Use produce that is as fresh as possible and at the peak of quality. Most vegetables should be used as soon as possible, but some fruits may require further ripening. Many tender fruits are picked before they are fully ripe, so wait a day or longer until the full flavour has developed. However, most fruits are best for preserving when they are slightly underripe.

Wash the food thoroughly to remove surface dirt and any traces of chemicals. Discard any bruised or mouldy fruit since microorganisms may have started to grow. Fruit with other surface blemishes or imperfections is fine to use.

Next read through the recipe and set out the ingredients. Remember to measure accurately.

2. Equipment Preparation

Partially fill a boiling-water canner with approximately the amount of hot water needed to cover the jars during processing. If food is to be processed less than 10 minutes, the jars need to be sterilized. Do this by boiling the jars for 10 minutes in the covered canner. Never put jars in the oven to sterilize. This exposes them to variations in temperature and may cause breakage. Jars do not need to be sterilized. when processing times are longer than 10 minutes, but they should be kept hot until they are filled. It is helpful to have an extra kettle of boiling water at hand in case the water level needs to be topped up after the filled jars are placed in the canner. If you live in an area with hard water, add a bit of vinegar to the water to prevent a film forming on the jars.

Place the metal disc part of the lids in boiling water for five minutes immediately before using. This sanitizes the lids and softens the sealing compound so an airtight seal is formed.

3. Filling Canning Jars

The processing time given in our recipes is based on the food being hot when it is put into the jars. It is important that the jars be processed immediately following the cooking stage.

A clean metal funnel is helpful to avoid spills when filling jars. Food may be ladled into the jar or poured using a small pitcher or measuring cup.

Leave a head space to allow for expansion of food during processing. For most foods, a head space of ½ inch (1 cm) is needed, although the head space may be as little as ¼ inch (5 mm) for sweet spreads. If the jars are too full, the food may boil out and interfere with the formation of the seal. Too much head space may result in the jar not sealing since the processing time is too short to drive out the extra air. We find it easiest to get in the habit of allowing ½ inch (1 cm) for all foods being processed.

Before placing a lid on the jar, be sure to remove any air trapped between pieces of food. Release any air bubbles by sliding a clean small wooden or plastic spatula between the food and the jar and gently move the food. Top up the liquid level if necessary after releasing the trapped air. Then wipe the rim of the jar with a clean cloth to remove any stickiness that could interfere with the formation of the seal.

Remove a metal disc from the boiling water and centre it on the jar rim. (Buy a magnetic lid lifter or glue a small magnet to the end of a wooden dowel rod to lift snap lids from the boiling water.) Then apply the screw band just until it is fingertip tight. Use only your fingertips! During processing, the air in the jar expands and is vented under the lid. When the jar cools, the air contracts and the lid "snaps" down, creating an airtight vacuum seal. If the lid is too tight, air cannot escape from the jar, possibly resulting in a failed seal.

4. Processing Canning Jars

Heating filled jars of food in boiling water for a specified time is called processing. Place the jars of filled food on the rack of a canner containing boiling water. Adjust the water level to cover the jars by approximately 1 inch (2.5 cm). Cover the canner and return to a boil. Start counting the processing time called for in the recipe when the water has returned to a steady boil. A kitchen timer is helpful for this. The processing time for each food is based on the size of the jar and the density and composition of the food, so follow times exactly. Under-processing can result in spoiled or off-flavoured food and over-processing may overcook the food. If you live at altitudes higher than 1,000 feet (306 meters), longer times are needed. Adjust the time as follows.

Adjustment for Processing at Higher Altitudes

At higher altitudes water boils at a lower temperature. So it is necessary to increase processing time if you live at higher elevations.

- Elevations between 1,000 and 3,000 feet (306 and 915 meters): add 5 minutes to the processing time given in the recipe.
- Elevations between 3,000 and 6,000 feet (916 and 1830 meters): add 10 minutes to the processing time given in the recipe.
- Elevations between 6,000 and 8,000 feet (1,830 and 2,440 meters): add 15 minutes to the processing time given in the recipe.
- Elevations between 8,000 and 10,000 feet (2,440 and 3,050 meters): add 20 minutes to the processing time given in the recipe.

5. Preserved Food Storage

When the processing is finished, turn off the heat and remove the jars from the canner. Use a jar lifter or lift the rack from the water by its handles. Transfer jars to a wooden cutting board or a surface covered with several layers of towels or newspapers. Do not place jars on a cold hard surface or they may break.

Do not tighten the seal; let the jars cool, undisturbed, for 12 to 24 hours. Then check the seal. It is easy to tell if the jars are sealed as the metal discs curve downwards. Refrigerate any jars that are not sealed for up to three weeks. Remove the screw bands, dry them and store separately. If you prefer, replace them loosely on the jar. The bands are not necessary for storage, as the firm seal achieved by the canning process is strong enough to keep the jar airtight.

When the jars are cool and you have checked the seals, attach labels with contents and date. Preserved foods are best kept in a dark, cool place. Light may cause food to darken and a heat source, such as hot pipes, a furnace or stove, may hasten the loss of quality. A dark closet or a storage area in the basement is ideal.

If our recipes and canning procedures are followed carefully, there should be no problem with spoilage. However, when you open a jar of preserved food, it is a good idea to look closely for any sign of spoilage like a bulging lid or any leakage. The lid should be tight and give resistance when opened. If the lid is loose, or if the food has any off-flavours or mould on the surface, the food must be discarded. Don't take any chances. Plan to use preserved foods within a year. As long as the seal is secure, there is no risk of spoilage for a much longer time, but the quality of the food will deteriorate with extended storage.

Equipment for Safe Boiling-Water Canning

1. Boiling-Water Canner

A boiling-water canner is a large covered container generally made from steel-covered enamel or stainless steel. A rack fits inside to hold the jars, keeping them from touching one another and elevating them from the bottom of the canner to allow water to circulate freely around them. The canner must be deep enough to allow at least 1 inch (2.5 cm) of briskly boiling water to cover the filled jars and the diameter should be no more than 4 inches (10 cm) wider than the burner on the stove.

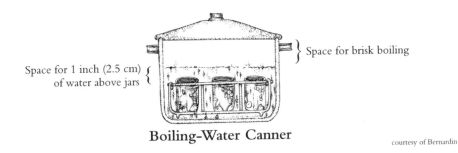

Space for brisk boiling

Space for 1 inch (2.5 cm) of water above jars

Boiling-Water Canner

courtesy of Bernardin

Any large cooking pot can be used for a canner as long as it has a tight-fitting lid and is large enough to hold the jars. A rack is essential for adequate circulation of water around the jars. A round cake rack can serve this purpose. If the rack does not have handles, you will need a jar lifter for removing the jars from the hot water.

2. Canning Jars and Lids

Before you start a recipe, be sure you have enough clean canning jars that are free from cracks or nicks. Canning jars, commonly called mason jars, are designed to withstand the temperatures of boiling-water canning. They are available in a variety of shapes and sizes from small ½ cup (125 mL) to large two quart (2 L) jars. Our recipes are designed for small batches, so we generally use the half-pint (250 mL) and pint (500 mL) sizes.

Jars have two sizes of lids, standard and wide mouth. The standard size is most commonly used, but wide-mouthed jars are useful for packing foods in larger pieces, such as dill pickles. Lids are made in two pieces, a metal disc and a screw band to keep the disc in place. The disc has a sealing compound that allows it to form a seal with the jar. Each disc, often called a "snap lid," is used one time only to ensure a proper jar seal. The screw band can be reused.

Possible Causes for Seal Failure or Spoiled Food

- Food was not processed in the canner for the correct time. It is important to start counting processing time just after the water in the canner returns to a boil.
- Processing time was not adjusted for altitude (see page 6).
- New sealing discs were not used or were not softened in boiling water.
- Screw bands were put on too tight or were re-tightened after processing.
- Too much or insufficient head space was left in the jar.
- The jar was cracked before, during or after processing. Cracking during processing could result from adding cold water to a canner of filled jars, placing hot jars on a cold surface or using jars not designed to withstand boiling-water temperatures.
- The quantity of ingredients called for in the recipe were not measured accurately.
- The vinegar was not of the standard 5% acetic acid. Always use vinegars of known acidity for canning purposes. For more about vinegars, see page 174.

Sweet
Spreads

Sweet Spreads

MAKING sweet spreads is synonymous with creative home-making. Using the many different fruits available throughout the year, the variety and marvellous flavours of your homemade sweet spreads will greatly exceed those of even the best commercial jams and spreads. In the following pages is a selection of spreads that feature exciting fruit combinations not even considered by commercial jam makers. Try them to liven up your breakfast table. And a gift jar of a homemade jam or other sweet spread is always appreciated. Remember to include the recipe with it.

Name That Spread!

Jams, preserves, jellies, marmalades, conserves and fruit butters all share the same characteristic consistency, thanks to a gel formed by pectin. What makes them different from one another is the size or absence of fruit pieces, the method of cooking and the addition of other ingredients. Fruit curds are unique because they are the only spread in this category thickened by eggs.

Jam is a mixture of fruit and sugar made either from fruits that are high in pectin content or with added pectin. The fruit is usually chopped very finely or mashed.

A *preserve* is the same as a jam but the fruit is in larger pieces.

Jelly is the same as jam except that the cooked fruit has been strained to give a clear spread. Jellies are usually made from fruits high in pectin or with added pectin.

Marmalade is a jam made from citrus fruit. Marmalades generally do not have pectin added since citrus rinds and seeds contain enough pectin to form a soft gel.

A *conserve* is a jam with the addition of nuts, dried fruits and often spices.

Fruit butter is a sweet spread made by cooking fruit pulp with sugar until it has a thick, smooth consistency with no liquid remaining. Spices are often added.

Fruit curd is a sweet spread made from citrus fruit, sugar, butter and eggs cooked gently until thickened.

Essential Sweet Spread Ingredients

Four ingredients are essential for making sweet spreads: fruit, sugar, pectin and acid. But it isn't enough that these four substances are present—the proportion between them is critical to forming a gel. Following tested recipes, such as the ones found in this book or those supplied by pectin manufacturers, gives the best chance of success. To add flavour we like to suggest such extras as small amounts of liqueurs, nuts, spices and citrus zest. Generally, these are added at the last minute just before bottling.

Fruit

Fruit for all sweet spreads should be firm and ripe and always of good quality. Never use overripe fruit, since pectin disappears as fruit ripens, resulting in a jam that may not form a gel. Slightly underripe fresh fruit contains the most pectin, especially important for making spreads with no added pectin. Irregular-shaped fruit or fruit that is scarred is perfectly good, but discard any that is spoiled or mouldy. Always wash or rinse fruit before use to remove any traces of dust, dirt or chemicals.

Fruit frozen without sugar is great for making jam and other sweet spreads. Plan to freeze such fruits as rhubarb, berries and cherries when they are plentiful to make into jam later at your convenience. Choose clean, slightly underripe fruits at the peak of the growing season. Place the fruit in single layers on shallow cookie trays in the quantities required for each recipe you plan to use. Freeze the trays of fruit and then package in airtight labelled containers. The natural flavour is better preserved by adding a small amount of sugar (note the amount for the quantity of fruit so you can subtract it later from the sugar called for in the recipe). When you use the frozen fruit to make a sweet spread, there is no need to defrost it first. Just use it in the recipe as you would fresh fruit.

Sugar

Sugar is a vital ingredient in all sweet spreads. It links with the pectin to form a gel and high concentrations prevent the growth of microorganisms. Sugar enhances the natural flavour of the fruit, so for that reason, a combination of a little sugar with an artificial sweetener is often used for our Light 'n' Low-Sugar Spreads (page 81).

Timing the addition of sugar affects the texture of the fruit used in sweet spreads. If fruit and sugar are simply cooked together, the fruit quickly breaks down. However, when sugar is combined with fruit for several hours before cooking, the fruit shrinks as part of its juice is drawn out. This partially dehydrated fruit keeps its shape in the finished spread. Our Elegant Oven Strawberry Jam (page 20) is a perfect example of this process.

Pectin

Pectin is a naturally occurring gum-like substance found in many fruits and vegetables. Fruits contain pectin in varying amounts depending on ripeness, variety and growing conditions. Pectin concentration is greatest in the cores, seeds and skins of the fruit and decreases considerably as the fruit ripens. Pectin molecules link with sugar and acid to form the gel that gives sweet spreads their smooth, semisolid consistency. Some fruits may have enough pectin to make spreads that set well, while others require added pectin.

Adding pectin to the fruit often produces a spread with a fresher taste, and it allows fully ripe fruit to be used. It also shortens cooking time since there is no need to concentrate the natural pectin before a gel can form. The set cooking time of added-pectin recipes means there is no question as to when the spread is done. And the yield from a given amount of fruit, often the most expensive ingredient, is greater because more pectin requires more sugar.

There are three ways to ensure enough pectin is available for making sweet spreads.

- **Commercial pectin:** Commercial pectin is a concentrated extract from high-pectin fruits such as apples and citrus fruits. It is available in liquid and powdered form, which are not interchangeable. Currently, only one manufacturer makes liquid pectin, and two brands of powdered fruit pectin are available. We have used both in testing our recipes. Be sure to check the "best before" date on the package.

- **Homemade apple pectin:** Make your own pectin extract from apples (page 25). This interesting source allows you to make a very small amount of jam with just a few pieces of fruit.

- **High-pectin/low-pectin fruits:** Combine high-pectin fruits with low pectin-ones to provide the required level of pectin. Adding apple to rhubarb or red currants to raspberries are good examples.

High-Pectin Fruits	Low-Pectin Fruits
apples (sour★ and sweet)	apricots★
cherries (sour★ and sweet)	blueberries
crabapples★	elderberries
cranberries★	figs
currants (red★ and black★)	nectarines
gooseberries★	peaches
grapefruit★	pears
grapes★	pineapple
kiwifruit★	raspberries★
lemons,★ limes★	rhubarb★
oranges★	strawberries★
plums (some kinds)★	
quinces	

Guide to Pectin Content of Fruits

Fruits marked with an asterisk (★) are high in the acid needed to combine with pectin for gel formation.

Acid

As well as having adequate pectin, fruit must contain the correct amount of acid to form a gel. Too much acid will form a gel that sets too quickly and too firmly, making the sweet spread "weep" as moisture is squeezed out. Marmalades often have too much acid so adding baking soda reduces their acidity. Too little acid prevents a gel from forming. Lemon juice is added to low-acid fruits to increase their acidity.

Gel Formation

The balance between fruit, sugar, pectin and acid is critical for gel formation. This balance is a delicate one, so it is essential to measure all ingredients accurately. Do not change the prescribed amounts, especially the amounts of sugar and acid. Always use tested recipes. Even then, a gel is not guaranteed, because the amounts of natural sugar, pectin and acid in the fruit vary due to weather and storage conditions. Some types of gels, especially in marmalades, may require several hours or even days for the pectin to set. Others form quickly, even before complete cooling. In general, marmalades and conserves form a lighter gel than jams and jellies. Do not make double recipes of sweet spreads as the longer cooking time required for a larger amount may cause the pectin to break down, preventing a gel from forming.

Tests for Determining When a Gel Will Form

There are two tests to determine when a sweet spread will form a gel.

Freezer Test

Place two small plates in the freezer ahead of time. Test for gel formation by putting a spoonful of hot fruit mixture on one chilled plate. Immediately return it to the freezer and wait for 2 minutes. Meanwhile, remove the saucepan from the heat source to prevent overcooking. If the mixture is sufficiently cooked, it will form a gel that moves slowly as the plate is tilted. If it doesn't form a gel, cook for another 2 minutes and repeat the test on the remaining chilled plate.

Sheet or Spoon Test

Begin cooking. Test for gel formation by periodically dipping a cool metal spoon into the hot fruit mixture and immediately lifting the spoon so the mixture runs off it. At first the drops will be light and syrupy. As the mixture continues to cook, the drops from the spoon will become heavier. When the mixture "sheets" from the spoon (the drops become very thick and two drops run together before dropping off), it will form a gel on cooling.

Spoon Test

Processing Sweet Spreads

Sweet spreads are processed by freezing or by 5-minute processing in a boiling-water canner. Detailed instructions for boiling-water processing are found on page 7. Note that sterilized mason jars with two-piece lids must be used to get an airtight seal when using the boiling-water procedure. Processing sweet spreads often allows the fruit to rise to the top. Stir before serving to break the gel and distribute the fruit. If not processed or frozen, sweet spreads may be stored in the refrigerator for up to 3 weeks.

For many years paraffin wax was used to seal jam jars, but it is no longer recommended. A layer of paraffin on top of a sweet spread does not give the necessary airtight seal. Moulds may grow in the small cracks and pinholes that occur as the wax cools. We used to think that simply removing any mould appearing on the sweet spread was sufficient to make it safe. However, research has since found that mould growth may produce harmful substances that can penetrate unseen throughout the jar. So invest in some of the attractive small canning jars that may be processed in a boiling-water bath. They are safe as well as pretty!

Essential Sweet Spread Equipment

A *large saucepan* is essential to allow the fruit mixture to come to a full rolling boil. It should be heavy to allow even distribution of heat and made of stainless steel or enamel to prevent reaction with the acid in the mixture. In our recipes, a "large saucepan" means one that holds approximately 4 quarts (4 L). A few of the larger recipes call for a "very large saucepan," meaning one that holds at least 6 quarts (6 L).

Sweet spreads should be preserved in mason jars closed with a screw band and a new metal disc. It is best to use half-cup (125 mL) or half-pint (250 mL) mason jars. Larger jars may produce a product with a softer gel since the longer cooling time of the larger quantity can cause breakdown of the gel.

You will also need a *boiling-water canner* with a rack for processing the fruit mixture, a *ladle or pitcher* for putting the fruit mixture into jars, and *tongs or lifters* for lifting the jars from the boiling water (unless the canner rack has handles).

Procedure for Shorter Time Boiling-Water Processing

Below is the step-by-step procedure for processing foods that require less than 10 minutes processing time. Use this procedure for all sweet spreads as directed in the recipes.

Shorter Time Processing Procedure

(For food that requires less than 10 minutes processing time.)

If the recipe requires a preparation and cooking time longer than 20 minutes, begin preparation of the ingredients first. Then bring the water and jars in the canner to a boil while the prepared food is cooking. If the ingredients require a shorter preparation and cooking time, begin heating the canner before you start your recipe. Remember the jars need to be sterilized before you fill them, which requires 10 minutes after the water reaches a boil. Have a kettle with boiling water handy to top up the water level in the canner after you have put in the jars.

Steps for Perfect Processing

20 Minutes Before Processing
Partially fill a boiling-water canner with hot water. Place in the canner a sufficient number of clean mason jars to hold the quantity of finished food prepared by the recipe. Cover and bring the water to a boil over high heat. Boil for at least 10 minutes to sterilize jars. This step generally requires 20 to 30 minutes, depending on the size of your canner.

5 Minutes Before Processing
Place snap lids in hot or boiling water approximately 5 minutes before you are ready to fill the jars. Follow the manufacturer's directions.

Filling Jars

Remove jars from canner and pour or ladle the foods into hot jars to within ½ inch (1 cm) of top rim (head space). If the food is in large pieces, remove trapped air bubbles by sliding a wooden or plastic spatula between glass and food; readjust the head space to ½ inch (1 cm). Wipe jar rim to remove any stickiness. Centre snap lid on jar; apply screw band just until fingertip tight.

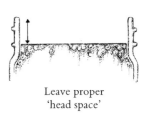

Leave proper 'head space'

Remove air bubbles

courtesy of Bernardin

Processing Jars

1. Place jars in canner and adjust water level to cover jars by 1 inch (2.5 cm). Cover canner and return water to boil. Begin timing when water returns to a boil. Process for 5 minutes.

2. Remove jars from canner to a surface covered with newspapers or with several layers of paper towels and cool for 24 hours. Check jar seals (sealed lids turn downward). Remove screw bands, dry and either replace loosely on jar or store separately. Label jars with contents and date and store in a cool, dark place.

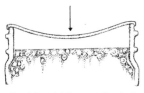

Cool jars 24 hours; check for vacuum seal.
Sealed lids curve downward

courtesy of Bernardin

Chapter One

Jams for All Seasons

G RACE your breakfast table with spreads few commercial jam-makers even think of. When you make your own, even the common ones are more concentrated and flavourful. You'll find nothing in a store to match our Peach Lavender Jam (page 29).

The wide variety of fruits available year-round make "in season" and "out of season" distinctions less important to home jam-makers. Even so, fresh, locally grown fruits at the peak of their growing season are still the most flavourful. But frequently we are simply too busy when local fruit is most plentiful to put all that we would like "under lids." So, let your trusty freezer save the day. Measure, bag and label fruits by recipe, then freeze. Make your frozen treasures into fresh-tasting jams during the long winter months. For example, tuck blueberries in your freezer to make Mango Blueberry Freezer Jam (page 38) when mangoes are plentiful and inexpensive. And there is no problem with using previously frozen fruit in a freezer jam that will again be frozen for longer storage. Several jams are non-seasonal. Winter Apricot Pineapple Jam and Australian Spiced Dried Fig Jam on pages 34 and 33 are wonderful any time of year.

In *Put A Lid On It!* we developed a recipe for Homemade Apple Pectin (page 25). This homemade pectin is ideal for making jams on the spur of the moment from small quantities of fruit. We have repeated it here and use it to make the small-batch jams found on page 26.

All recipes using powdered fruit pectin have been tested with both Certo Fruit Pectin Crystals and Bernardin Fruit Pectin. For more on pectin, see page 12.

Serving Suggestions

Add jam to some plain yogurt to make personalized fruit-flavoured yogurts. Or mix yogurt, jam and a ripe banana in a blender to make a refreshing smoothie. Jams can be used to make a quick trifle. Spread ladyfingers with jam and top with a custard sauce. Spoonfuls of jam are a perfect topping for a plain cheesecake or a filling for a jelly roll cake. And, of course, breakfast toast would be nothing without jam.

Tips

- A small amount of sugar added to fruit that is being frozen results in better flavour retention. But remember to reduce the sugar in your recipe by the amount added to the frozen fruit.

List of Recipes

Elegant Oven Strawberry Jam

An early version of this "amazingly successful" recipe appeared in *The Laura Secord Canadian Cookbook* published with the Canadian Home Economics Association in 1966 under the name of Sunshine Strawberry Jam. The briefly cooked berries were set in the sun for 2 to 3 days to allow evaporation. Modern convection ovens greatly speed up this process and avoid the problem of "crawlies" getting to the jam before it is finished.

8 cups	halved or quartered strawberries	2 L
4 cups	granulated sugar	1 L
¼ cup	balsamic vinegar or lemon juice	50 mL

1. Combine berries and sugar in a very large stainless steel or enamel saucepan. Let stand for 2 hours, stirring several times.
2. Add vinegar and bring to a boil over high heat; reduce heat and boil gently, uncovered, for 10 minutes.
3. Pour into two 13 x 9 inch (3.5 L) glass baking dishes and place in a convection or standard oven at 150°F (65°C). Bake until mixture is thickened and will form a gel,★ about 3 hours for convection and 10 hours for standard, stirring occasionally.
4. Ladle into sterilized jars and process as directed on page 16 (Shorter Time Processing Procedure).

Makes 4 cups (1 L).

Variation:

Herb Strawberry Jam
Insert a sprig of fresh mint or basil in each jar before filling with jam.

★ To determine when mixture will form a gel, see page 14.

Gingered Rhubarb Jam With Honey

In England it's traditional to combine ginger with rhubarb. In this jam, ginger adds a pungent spiciness while honey offsets rhubarb's strong tartness.

1	lemon	1
2 cups	chopped fresh or frozen rhubarb	500 mL
1	large tart apple, peeled, cored and finely chopped	1
½ cup	water	125 mL
1½ cups	granulated sugar	375 mL
1 cup	liquid honey	250 mL
1½ tbsp	finely chopped crystallized ginger (page 196)	20 mL

1. Remove thin outer rind from lemon with vegetable peeler and cut into fine strips with scissors or sharp knife; or use a zester. Place lemon rind in a large stainless steel or enamel saucepan. Squeeze juice from lemon and reserve 1 tbsp (15 mL).
2. Combine rhubarb, apple and water in a medium stainless steel or enamel saucepan. Bring to a boil over high heat, cover, reduce heat and boil gently for 15 minutes or until fruit is tender.
3. Add sugar, honey, ginger and reserved lemon juice. Return to a boil and boil rapidly, uncovered, until mixture will form a gel,★ about 8 minutes, stirring frequently. Remove from heat.
4. Ladle into sterilized jars and process as directed on page 16 (Shorter Time Processing Procedure).

Makes 3¼ cups (800 mL).

Tip: Freeze fresh rhubarb to use when it is not in season.

★ To determine when mixture will form a gel, see page 14.

Four-Fruit Red Jam

Use fresh or frozen fruit, but remember to measure frozen fruit before thawing and thaw before crushing.

2 cups	raspberries or loganberries, crushed	500 mL
2 cups	red currants, crushed	500 mL
2 cups	sliced strawberries, crushed	500 mL
1½ cups	chopped sour cherries	375 mL
4 cups	granulated sugar	1 L
¼ cup	lemon juice	50 mL

1. Place raspberries, currants, strawberries, cherries, sugar and lemon juice in a large stainless steel or enamel saucepan. Cover and let stand for 10 minutes.
2. Bring to a boil over high heat, stirring constantly. Boil rapidly, uncovered, until mixture will form a gel,★ about 15 minutes, stirring frequently. Remove from heat.
3. Ladle into sterilized jars and process as directed on page 16 (Shorter Time Processing Procedure).

Makes about 5 cups (1.25 L).

Red Fruit Sauce

This one is excellent for pancakes, French toast or waffles.
Melt ½ cup (125 mL) Four-Fruit Red Jam in a small saucepan over low heat. Stir 1 tsp (5 mL) cornstarch into ½ cup (125 mL) cherry juice and ¼ cup (50 mL) water. Whisk into melted jam, boil gently, uncovered, over low heat until slightly thickened. Stir in ½ tsp (2 mL) ground cinnamon, a small amount of grated lemon rind and ½ cup (125 mL) sour cherries. Makes about 1¾ cups (425 mL).

★ To determine when mixture will form a gel, see page 14.

Pear Raspberry Jam

Make this jam at just about any time of the year. Good pears are available almost all year round and the raspberries in this recipe are frozen. Pear Raspberry Jam can give a fresh addition to your jam shelf when other fresh jam ingredients are scarce.

6	medium pears, peeled, cored and chopped	6
1	pkg (425 g) frozen raspberries in light syrup, thawed	1
6 cups	granulated sugar	1.5 L
2 tsp	grated lemon rind	10 mL
2 tbsp	lemon juice	25 mL
1	pouch (85 mL) liquid fruit pectin	1

1. Place pears, raspberries, sugar, lemon rind and juice in a large stainless steel or enamel saucepan. Bring to a full boil over high heat and boil hard for 2 minutes, stirring constantly. Remove from heat and stir in pectin.
2. Ladle into sterilized jars and process as directed on page 16 (Shorter Time Processing Procedure).

Makes 6 cups (1.5 L).

Sour Cherry Gooseberry Jam

Tart sour cherries complement the sweet gooseberries wonderfully in this simple recipe.

2 cups	chopped pitted sour cherries	500 mL
	(about 4 cups/1 L whole fruit)	
2 cups	chopped gooseberries	500 mL
	(about 2½ cups/625 mL whole fruit)	
1 cup	water	250 mL
4 cups	granulated sugar	1 L

1. Combine cherries, gooseberries and water in a large stainless steel or enamel saucepan. Bring to a boil, reduce heat, cover and boil gently for 15 minutes.
2. Add sugar, return to a full boil and boil rapidly, uncovered, until mixture will form a gel,★ about 15 minutes, stirring frequently. Remove from heat.
3. Ladle into sterilized jars and process as directed on page 16 (Shorter Time Processing Procedure).

Makes 4 cups (1 L).

Variation:

Ginger Sour Cherry Gooseberry Jam
Add 2 tbsp (25 mL) chopped crystallized ginger in Step 2.

Fruit Fool
Summer fruits shine in jams and so why not allow them to come forth and shine again in a fruit fool. Most fools are silky-smooth yet oh-so-simple to make.
Whip 1 cup (250 mL) whipping cream in a medium bowl with an electric mixer until firm, but not stiff peaks. Gently fold in ½ cup (125 mL) your choice of jam, 2 tbsp (25 mL) Apricot Brandy (page 199) or orange liqueur, and 1 tsp (5 mL) grated lemon zest. Serve immediately or refrigerate for a few hours. Makes 4 to 6 servings.

★ To determine when mixture will form a gel, see page 14.

Small-Batch Jams

The Homemade Apple Pectin in *Put a Lid on It!* was so popular we decided to include it again. Keep a supply of this apple pectin on hand to make many different jams in very short order with whatever fruit is available. We have included a recipe for Sweet Cherry Jam to get you started and offer some suggestions for other fruit combinations. Use your imagination to combine your favourite fruits with an equal amount of Homemade Apple Pectin for your own signature breakfast spread.

Homemade Apple Pectin

The pectin content of apples decreases during storage, so remember to make this pectin in the fall when apples are at their freshest. The straining process is made easier if the apple mixture is first pressed through a coarse sieve to remove most of the solids and then strained through several layers of cheesecloth or a jelly bag for extra clarity.

7	tart apples (about 2 lb/1 kg)	7
4 cups	water	1 L
2 tbsp	lemon juice	25 mL

1. Cut apples into quarters (do not peel or core). Combine with water and lemon juice in a large stainless steel or enamel saucepan. Bring to a boil over high heat, cover, reduce heat and simmer for 40 minutes, stirring occasionally.
2. Strain through a coarse sieve and discard solids. Then pour liquid through a jelly bag or several layers of cheesecloth.
3. Ladle into sterilized jars and process as directed on page 16 (Shorter Time Processing Procedure).

Makes 4 cups (1 L).

Small-Batch Jams Using Homemade Apple Pectin

1. For each 1 cup (250 mL) finely chopped fruit (see list below), add 1 cup (250 mL) Homemade Apple Pectin and ¾ cup (175 mL) granulated sugar.
2. Combine fruit, pectin and sugar in a stainless steel or enamel saucepan. Add 1 tsp (5 mL) lemon juice if fruit is low acid (see chart on page 13). Bring to a boil over high heat and boil rapidly, uncovered, until mixture will form a gel,★ about 10 to 15 minutes, stirring frequently.
3. Ladle into jars, cover and store in refrigerator for up to 3 weeks. If desired, process as directed on page 16 (Shorter Time Processing Procedure).

Suggested Jam Combinations:
Each recipe makes about 1¼ cups (300 mL) jam.
Follow the above recipe using one of the following:

- ½ cup (125 mL) chopped kiwifruit and ½ cup (125 mL) chopped mango.
- ½ cup (125 mL) chopped pears and ½ cup (125 mL) chopped blueberries.
- ½ cup (125 mL) chopped fresh pineapple and ½ cup (125 mL) chopped papaya.
- ½ cup (125 mL) chopped blueberries and ½ cup (125 mL) chopped plums.
- 1 cup (250 mL) frozen raspberries, thawed and mashed, with 1 tsp (5 mL) chopped mint stirred in after cooking.

Small-Batch Sweet Cherry Jam

Sweet cherries can be expensive even in season but this small-batch jam requires only slightly more than a half pound of cherries.

1 cup	Homemade Apple Pectin	250 mL
1 cup	chopped sweet cherries	250 mL
	(about 10 oz/280 g)	
½ tsp	lemon juice	2 mL
¾ cup	granulated sugar	175 mL

Makes 1¼ cups (300 mL).

★ To determine when mixture will form a gel, see page 14.

Fresh Fig And Strawberry Jam

This jam is so good it disappears from the shelf. The fresh figs lend an amazing texture and taste to the strawberries. Be sure to make as much of it as jar and cupboard space allows whenever you can get your hands on fresh figs. Otherwise you may be like Margaret—she raved about it and then gave away so many jars she didn't have any left for herself!

1 lb	fresh green figs, stemmed and cut into small pieces	500 g
2 cups	quartered strawberries	500 mL
2 cups	granulated sugar	500 mL
3 tbsp	lemon juice	45 mL

1. Place figs, strawberries, sugar and lemon juice in a medium stainless steel or enamel saucepan. Cover and let stand for 1 hour, stirring occasionally.
2. Bring to a boil over high heat, reduce heat to medium and boil rapidly, uncovered, until mixture will form a gel,★ about 15 minutes, stirring frequently. Remove from heat.
3. Ladle into sterilized jars and process as directed on page 16 (Shorter Time Processing Procedure).

Makes about 4 cups (1 L).

Tip: Fresh figs have a longer season than we realized. We asked a specialty green grocer who told us they start arriving in Canada from California in May, and from Greece and Italy in late summer and fall. If you missed them, occasionally you can find figs from South America in the late fall and early winter. Remember that fresh figs are extremely perishable and should be used as soon as possible after purchase. They may be stored in a refrigerator for up to 3 days.

★ To determine when mixture will form a gel, see page 14.

Fresh Apricot Jam

This very easy-to-make recipe produces a lovely fresh-tasting jam. It may be all that is needed to spur a neophyte's interest in jam-making.

3 cups	coarsely chopped unpeeled fresh apricots	750 mL
	(about 2 lb/1 kg, or 14 to 20 apricots)	
3½ cups	granulated sugar	875 mL
¼ cup	lemon juice	50 mL

1. Stir together apricots, sugar and lemon juice in a large bowl. Cover and let stand at room temperature for 12 hours, stirring occasionally.
2. Place apricot mixture in a large stainless steel or enamel saucepan. Bring to a boil over high heat, stirring frequently. Reduce heat to medium and boil rapidly, uncovered, until mixture will form a gel,★ about 25 minutes, stirring frequently. Remove from heat.
3. Ladle into sterilized jars and process as directed on page 16 (Shorter Time Processing Procedure).

Makes about 3½ cups (875 mL).

Crunchy Apricot Breakfast Yogurt
In small bowl, combine 1 cup (250 mL) low-fat plain or vanilla yogurt. Stir in ½ cup (125 mL) Fresh Apricot Jam. Stir in 1 cup (250 mL) granola-type cereal just before serving. Makes about 2 cups (500 mL).

★ To determine when mixture will form a gel, see page 14.

Australian Spiced Dried Fig Jam (page 33) and Winter Apricot Pineapple Jam (page 34) are just a few of the thrilling combinations featured in Jams for All Seasons.

Peach Lavender Jam

Margaret was a judge at the 1998 Royal Winter Fair, which is held each November in Toronto. Yvonne Tremblay, a Toronto food consultant, won the Grand Champion Jam and Jelly contest with this marvellous peach jam recipe. She commented that many people do not think of cooking with lavender, an edible herb that subtly accents the flavour of fresh fruits such as peaches, strawberries, raspberries, orange and lemon.

2 tbsp	dried lavender flowers	25 mL
½ cup	boiling water	125 mL
4 cups	finely chopped peaches, about 5-6 medium	1 L
2 tbsp	lemon juice	25 mL
6 cups	granulated sugar	1.5 L
1	pouch (85 mL) liquid fruit pectin Dried lavender flowers (see Tip)	1

1. Place lavender flowers in a small bowl. Pour boiling water over flowers and steep for 20 minutes. Strain and discard flowers.
2. Combine lavender liquid, peaches, lemon juice and sugar in a large stainless steel or enamel saucepan. Bring to a full boil over high heat and boil hard for 2 minutes, stirring constantly. Remove from heat and stir in pectin.
3. Ladle into sterilized jars and process as directed on page 16 (Shorter Time Processing Procedure).

Makes 6 cups (1.5 L).

Tip: Yvonne has suggested looking for organically grown lavender at herb fairs and herb specialty growers. For an added touch, place a small sprig on top of jam before sealing.

To offer a more exotic strawberry jam for tea, turn to page 27.

Spiced Wine Peach Jam

Spices and wine do interesting flavourful things to ordinary peaches in this sophisticated jam.

½ cup	golden raisins	125 mL
⅓ cup	dry red wine or juice (see Tip)	75 mL
4 cups	finely chopped peaches	1 L
	(5 to 6 medium peaches)	
3 tbsp	lemon juice	45 mL
1	box (57 g) powdered fruit pectin	1
5 cups	granulated sugar	1.25 L
1 tsp	ground cinnamon	5 mL
½ tsp	ground allspice	2 mL

1. Bring raisins and wine to a boil in a small saucepan, remove from heat, drain and discard liquid.
2. Combine raisins, peaches, lemon juice and pectin in a large stainless steel or enamel saucepan. Bring to a boil over high heat, stirring constantly. Add sugar, return to a full boil and boil hard for 1 minute, stirring constantly. Remove from heat and stir in cinnamon and allspice.
3. Ladle into sterilized jars and process as directed on page 16 (Shorter Time Processing Procedure).

Makes about 6 cups (1.5 L).

Variation:

Spiced Wine Pear Jam
Replace peaches with 4 cups (1 L) finely chopped pears. Ground nutmeg is an excellent substitution for the cinnamon.

Tip: Wine can be replaced with pineapple or orange juice.

Festive Cranstrawberry Jam

This jam's ruby-rich appearance is just right with festive Christmas food. It adds great colour to your breakfast table and wonderful taste to toast and muffins all year round.

1	pkg (425 g) frozen sliced strawberries in light syrup, thawed	1
2 cups	fresh or frozen cranberries	500 mL
1	large unpeeled orange, cut into large pieces	1
3 cups	granulated sugar	750 mL
1	pouch (85 mL) liquid fruit pectin	1
2 tbsp	orange liqueur or frozen orange juice concentrate	25 mL

1. Place strawberries in a medium stainless steel or enamel saucepan.
2. Coarsely chop cranberries and orange in a food processor. Remove and add to saucepan. Stir in sugar. Bring to a full boil over high heat and boil hard for 2 minutes, stirring constantly. Remove from heat and stir in pectin and liqueur.
3. Ladle into sterilized jars and process as directed on page 16 (Shorter Time Processing Procedure).

Makes 6 cups (1.5 L).

Cinnamon Tortilla Roll-ups

An interesting use for this jam as well as many others.

Warm a small flour tortilla in either the microwave oven or in a nonstick skillet. Mix 1 tbsp (15 mL) each: low-fat plain yogurt, low-fat ricotta cheese and 1 tsp (5 mL) Festive Cranstrawberry Jam. Spread mixture evenly over tortilla, add a dash of ground cinnamon or nutmeg, roll up and enjoy!

Honeydew Lemon Ginger Jam

Honeydew, lemon and ginger give this jam its refreshing unique flavour.

2	large lemons	2
1 cup	water	250 mL
2½ cups	chopped honeydew melon (about 1 lb/500 g)	625 mL
2 cups	granulated sugar	500 mL
⅓ cup	finely chopped crystallized ginger (page 196)	75 mL

1. Remove thin outer rind from lemons with vegetable peeler and cut into fine strips with scissors or sharp knife; or use a zester. Place in a large stainless steel or enamel saucepan. Squeeze juice from lemons and measure ½ cup (125 mL). Cut remaining white rinds into quarters. Add juice, white rind pieces and water to saucepan. Bring to a boil over high heat, reduce heat, cover and boil gently for 20 minutes or until rind is soft. Use tongs to remove and discard white rind pieces.
2. Add melon, sugar and ginger. Return to a boil and boil rapidly, uncovered, until mixture will form a gel,★ about 10 minutes, stirring frequently. Remove from heat.
3. Ladle into sterilized jars and process as directed on page 16 (Shorter Time Processing Procedure).

Makes 2½ cups (625 mL).

Jam Chutney
A fresh-tasting jam with a few additions can produce a chutney in short order.
Cook 1 onion, chopped, with a small amount of water in a medium saucepan until soft. Add 1 cup (250 mL) jam, ¼ cup (50 mL) vinegar, ¼ tsp (1 mL) each: salt and curry powder. Add a dash of cinnamon or cloves to taste. Boil gently until thickened. Makes about 1 cup (250 mL).

★ To determine when mixture will form a gel, see page 14.

Australian Spiced Dried Fig Jam

Fig lovers will enjoy this succulent spread that Ellie discovered while in Australia.

8 oz	dried figs★	250 g
2¼ cups	water	550 mL
4½ cups	granulated sugar	1.125 L
¼ tsp	ground cinnamon	1 mL
¼ tsp	ground nutmeg	1 mL
1	box (57 g) powdered fruit pectin	1
1 tsp	grated lemon rind	5 mL
¼ cup	lemon juice	50 mL

1. Combine figs and water in a medium bowl. Let stand for 8 hours or overnight.
2. Drain figs, reserving liquid. Remove and discard stems and chop fruit finely. Place chopped fruit in a 4 cup (1 L) liquid measure and add reserved liquid and enough water to bring level to 3 cups (750 mL).
3. Combine sugar, cinnamon and nutmeg in a bowl. Set aside.
4. Place fig mixture, pectin, lemon rind and juice in a large stainless steel or enamel saucepan. Bring to a boil over high heat, stirring constantly. Add sugar-spice mixture, return to a full boil and boil hard for 1 minute, stirring constantly. Remove from heat.
5. Ladle into sterilized jars and process as directed on page 16 (Shorter Time Processing Procedure).

Makes 5 cups (1.25 L).

★ Since figs come in a variety of package sizes, it is important to check the weight.

Winter Apricot Pineapple Jam

This surprisingly tasty jam is as easy to make as opening two cans and adding a bit of sugar and pectin. Try it when fresh fruit is out of season.

1	can (14 oz/398 mL) apricot halves in light syrup	1
1	can (14 oz/398 mL) pineapple pieces in own juice	1
3½ cups	granulated sugar	875 mL
1½ tbsp	lemon juice	20 mL
1	pouch (85 mL) liquid fruit pectin	1

1. Drain apricots and pineapple, reserving juice if desired. Chop fruit finely in a food processor or by hand.
2. Combine fruit, sugar and lemon juice in a large stainless steel or enamel saucepan. Bring to a full boil over high heat and boil hard for 2 minutes. Remove from heat and stir in pectin.
3. Ladle into sterilized jars and process as directed on page 16 (Shorter Time Processing Procedure).

Makes 4 cups (1 L).

Tip: Use liquid drained from fruit to sweeten beverages such as tea or lemonade or combine with plain gelatin for a simple dessert.

Pineapple Orange Rosemary Freezer Jam

The flavour of fresh pineapple combines wonderfully with orange and rosemary to make a delightful golden spread. Fold into plain yogurt for a quick and simple dessert.

3½ cups	granulated sugar	875 mL
1	sweet orange	1
1¼ cups	finely chopped fresh pineapple	300 mL
1	pouch (85 mL) liquid fruit pectin	1
4	sprigs fresh rosemary	4

1. Place sugar in an ovenproof shallow pan and warm in a 250°F (120°C) oven for 15 minutes. (Warm sugar dissolves better.)
2. Remove thin outer rind from orange with vegetable peeler and cut into fine strips with scissors or sharp knife; or use a zester. Squeeze juice from orange. Place orange rind and juice in a large bowl. Stir in pineapple and sugar and let stand for 10 minutes, stirring occasionally.
3. Stir in pectin, stirring constantly for 3 minutes.
4. Insert a sprig of rosemary into each jar or plastic container. Ladle jam into jars to within ½ inch (1 cm) of rim. Cover with tight-fitting lids. Label jars and let stand at room temperature until set, up to 24 hours.
5. Refrigerate for up to 3 weeks or freeze for longer storage.

Makes 4 cups (1 L).

Kiwifruit Raspberry Freezer Jam

This colourful combination produces a handsome jam. Fresh mint adds a refreshing note.

3½ cups	granulated sugar	875 mL
1 cup	crushed fresh or frozen raspberries	250 mL
¾ cup	finely chopped kiwifruit	175 mL
1	pouch (85 mL) liquid fruit pectin	1
2 tbsp	finely chopped fresh mint (optional)	25 mL
1 tbsp	lemon juice	15 mL

1. Place sugar in an ovenproof shallow pan and warm in a 250°F (120°C) oven for 15 minutes. (Warm sugar dissolves better.)
2. Place raspberries and kiwifruit in a large bowl. Stir in sugar and let stand for 10 minutes, stirring occasionally.
3. Add pectin, mint and lemon juice, stirring constantly for 3 minutes.
4. Ladle jam into clean jars or plastic containers to within ½ inch (1 cm) of rim. Cover with tight-fitting lids. Label jars and let stand at room temperature until set, up to 24 hours.
5. Refrigerate for up to 3 weeks or freeze for longer storage.

Makes 4 cups (1 L).

Variation:

Kiwifruit Loganberry Freezer Jam
Replace raspberries with same amount of loganberries.

Tip: Use a potato masher to crush fruit. Using a food processor will overprocess it.

Pear and Cranberry Freezer Jam

This jam's zippy flavour nicely complements scones or cheese tea biscuits.

4 cups	granulated sugar	1 L
3	Bartlett pears, peeled, cored and chopped	3
2 cups	fresh or frozen cranberries, finely chopped	500 mL
2 tsp	grated lemon rind	10 mL
2 tbsp	lemon juice	25 mL
1	pouch (85 mL) liquid fruit pectin	1

1. Place sugar in an ovenproof shallow pan and warm in a 250°F (120°C) oven for 15 minutes. (Warm sugar dissolves better.)
2. Combine pears, cranberries, lemon rind and sugar in a large bowl and let stand for 10 minutes, stirring occasionally.
3. Add lemon juice and pectin, stirring constantly for 3 minutes.
4. Ladle jam into clean jars or plastic containers to within ½ inch (1 cm) of rim. Cover with tight-fitting lids. Label jars and let stand at room temperature until set, up to 24 hours.
5. Refrigerate for up to 3 weeks or freeze for longer storage.

Makes 4½ cups (1.125 L).

Mango Blueberry Freezer Jam

Capture the fragrant, exotic, sweet-tart flavour of mangoes and combine it with the rich blue colour of blueberries in this ambrosial jam. Folded into plain yogurt or spooned over a pudding, it makes a super simple dessert.

2¾ cups	granulated sugar	675 mL
1 cup	finely chopped mangoes	250 mL
	(about 2 mangoes)	
¾ cup	chopped blueberries, fresh or frozen	175 mL
1 tsp	finely grated orange rind	5 mL
1	pouch (85 mL) liquid fruit pectin	1
1½ tbsp	lemon juice	20 mL

1. Place sugar in an ovenproof shallow pan and warm in a 250°F (120°C) oven for 15 minutes. (Warm sugar dissolves better.)
2. Combine mangoes, blueberries, orange rind and sugar in a large bowl and let stand for 10 minutes, stirring occasionally.
3. Add pectin and lemon juice, stirring constantly for 3 minutes.
4. Ladle jam into clean jars or plastic containers to within ½ inch (1 cm) of rim. Cover with tight-fitting lids. Label jars and let stand at room temperature until set, up to 24 hours.
5. Refrigerate for up to 3 weeks or freeze for longer storage.

Makes 3½ cups (875 mL).

Tip: To cut a mango, set it upright on a cutting board with the narrow side facing you. Slice off one side, just clearing the long flat seed. Repeat on the opposite side. Using a paring knife, carefully cut the flesh from the skin in a single piece, keeping as close to the skin as possible. Peel skin from the fruit left on the seed, then cut off the flesh.

Variation:

Mango Saskatoon Berry Freezer Jam
Replace blueberries with same amount of Saskatoon berries.

Microwave Ginger Plum Jam

Microwave purple plums anytime they are available for this small-batch, ginger-spiked jam. It takes about half an hour to prepare. Make a wonderful plum glaze for oven-roasted salmon by melting some of the jam and brushing it on the salmon while it is roasting.

3 cups	chopped purple plums	750 mL
	(about 10 to 12 plums)	
2 cups	granulated sugar	500 mL
4 tsp	lemon juice	20 mL
¼ cup	finely chopped crystallized ginger	50 mL
	(page 196)	

1. Place plums and sugar in a deep 8 cup (2 L) microwavable container. Stir in lemon juice.
2. Microwave, uncovered, on High (100%) for 7 minutes, stirring twice. Add ginger; microwave, uncovered, on High for 15 to 18 minutes or until mixture will form a gel,★ stirring every 4 minutes.
3. Ladle into sterilized jars and process as directed on page 16 (Shorter Time Processing Procedure).

Makes 2½ cups (625 mL).

Tip: Each summer, plums arrive in our markets in great variety—bright yellow and green (best known as greengage), iridescent red and dark purple. One fresh plum contains about 35 calories, which compares with 81 calories in a fresh apple and 100 in a fresh pear or banana. Plums are a very good low-calorie snack.

★ To determine when mixture will form a gel, see page 14.

Microwave Brandied Apricot Jam

Brandy heightens the flavour of this multipurpose jam. It's always an excellent spread for your morning toast, but you can use it anytime you need an apricot glaze … for a fresh fruit tart or to brush on spareribs, pork roast or chicken.

1¼ cups	dried apricots (about 8 oz/250 g)	300 mL
1½ cups	water	375 mL
2 tbsp	lemon juice	25 mL
1	box (57 g) powdered fruit pectin	1
3 cups	granulated sugar	750 mL
¼ cup	brandy	50 mL

1. Combine apricots and water in a medium bowl. Let stand for 4 hours or overnight.
2. Drain liquid from apricots into a large 3 quart (3 L) microwavable covered container. Finely chop apricots in a food processor or by hand. Add apricots, lemon juice and pectin to container. Microwave, covered, on High (100%) for 6 minutes or until mixture comes to a boil, stirring twice.
3. Add sugar. Microwave, uncovered, on High for 5 minutes or until mixture returns to a full boil and boil hard for 1 minute. Stir in brandy.
4. Ladle into sterilized jars and process as directed on page 16 (Shorter Time Processing Procedure).

Makes 4 cups (1 L).

Microwave Peach Jam with Orange Liqueur

Intense peach flavour is highlighted by orange in this elegant and attractive jam.

3 cups	chopped fresh or frozen peaches	750 mL
2 cups	granulated sugar	500 mL
2 tbsp	lemon juice	25 mL
2 tbsp	orange liqueur or frozen orange juice concentrate, thawed	25 mL

1. Place peaches and sugar in a deep 8 cup (2 L) microwavable container. Stir in lemon juice.
2. Microwave, uncovered, on High (100%) for 7 minutes, stirring twice. Microwave, uncovered, on High for 12 to 15 minutes or until mixture will form a gel,★ stirring every 4 minutes. Stir in liqueur.
3. Ladle into sterilized jars and process as directed on page 16 (Shorter Time Processing Procedure).

Makes 2 cups (500 mL).

Tip: If peaches are still frozen, you may need to add 2 to 3 minutes to the total cooking time.

Peach Shake
A marvellous shake is easily made using this jam.
Place 1 cup (250 mL) vanilla frozen yogurt, ½ cup (125 mL) orange juice and ¼ cup (50 mL) Microwave Peach Jam with Orange Liqueur in a blender container. Process until smooth. Add milk or plain yogurt if you prefer a less thick shake.

★ To determine when mixture will form a gel, see page 14.

Chapter Two

Jellies Made Easy

T HE BEST THING about making jellies is their easy preparation—no peeling or coring fruits, just wash, chop and use the lot. Then cook the fruit and strain through a jelly bag. Add sugar to the strained juice and cook until a gel stage is reached (more about this on page 16). A crystal clear, sparkling jelly is the happy result.

Many of our recipes make jelly-making even easier. They use prepared juice so there is no need for washing, chopping or straining. Peach Amaretto Jelly with Almonds (page 47) uses frozen peach nectar. Apple Cider Cinnamon Jelly (page 51) starts with fresh apple cider. Jellies made from juices that have not been cooked with their skins and seeds require added pectin to form a gel. Our Homemade Apple Pectin (see page 25) is used in Grape or Cranberry Thyme Jelly and Citrus Breakfast Jelly, on page 45.

The only equipment needed for jelly-making that is not required for jams is a jelly bag to strain the cooked fruit mixture. It is made of fabric with a sufficiently close weave to remove enough fruit pulp to ensure a clear jelly. You can buy one or you can line a colander or strainer with several layers of cheesecloth or an unused all-purpose cloth. Set the colander over a large bowl, pour in the fruit mixture and allow it to stand until the juice has drained through. This process can require up to several hours, but if you first press the fruit pulp through a coarse sieve to remove the larger solids, the resulting liquid will flow through the cloth much more quickly. The secret to a clear jelly is to let the juice drain through the cloth on its own. Avoid the temptation to squeeze out that last little bit of juice!

Serving Suggestions

There are as many uses for jellies as there are jellies. Our Tropical Fruit Jelly and Red Currant and Raspberry Jelly (pages 48 and 49) are right at home on a muffin, tea biscuit or piece of toast. Others, such as Cranberry Thyme Jelly (page 45) are great as meat condiments. Jalapeño Mint Jelly (page 50) and White Wine Jelly with Roasted Sweet Peppers (page 52) partner with Cheddar or cream cheese and crackers.

Give a jar of sparkling jelly as a hostess gift. Wrap it in a square of cellophane tied just above the lid and include the recipe.

List of Recipes

Small-Batch Jellies

Using commercial juices in these small-batch recipes eliminates the chopping and straining usually associated with jelly-making.

Small-Batch Jellies Using Homemade Apple Pectin

Be adventurous and create your own jelly recipe. Use your choice of fruit juice with an equal quantity of Homemade Apple Pectin. Here's how:

1. For each 1 cup (250 mL) fruit juice, add 1 cup (250 mL) Homemade Apple Pectin (page 25) and ¾ cup (175 mL) granulated sugar.
2. Combine juice, pectin and sugar in a medium stainless steel or enamel saucepan. Add 1 tsp (5 mL) lemon juice if fruit is low acid (see chart on page 13). Bring to a boil over high heat and boil rapidly, uncovered, stirring constantly, until mixture will form a gel,★ about 12 to 15 minutes.
3. Ladle into jars, cover and store in refrigerator for up to 3 weeks.

Suggested Jellies:
Each recipe makes about 1 cup (250 mL) jelly. If desired, process as directed on page 16 (Shorter Time Processing Procedure).

Follow the above recipe using one of the following:
- 1 cup (250 mL) white grape juice
- 1 cup (250 mL) port, sherry or white wine
- 1 cup (250 mL) fruit juice cocktail

★ To determine when mixture will form a gel, see page 14.

Small-Batch Citrus Breakfast Jelly

Fresh citrus juices give this jelly a wonderful refreshing flavour. You can substitute frozen or bottled juices for fresh. Strain juice to give a sparkling appearance.

1 cup	Homemade Apple Pectin (page 25)	250 mL
½ cup	fresh orange juice	125 mL
½ cup	fresh grapefruit juice	125 mL
¾ cup	granulated sugar	175 mL

1. Combine pectin, orange juice, grapefruit juice and sugar in a medium stainless steel or enamel saucepan. Bring to a boil over high heat and boil rapidly, uncovered, until mixture will form a gel,★ about 15 minutes, stirring frequently. Remove from heat.
2. Ladle into jars, cover and store in refrigerator for up to 3 weeks.

Makes 1 cup (250 mL).

Variations:

Grape or Cranberry Thyme Jelly
Use 1 cup (250 mL) pure grape juice or cranberry juice in place of grapefruit and orange juices. Insert a sprig of fresh thyme into each jar before filling.

★ To determine when mixture will form a gel, see page 14.

Lemon Rosemary Jelly

A light refreshing jelly, it complements lamb and chicken. When melted, it makes a perfect glaze for a fruit tart or barbecued ribs.

2	large lemons	2
2½ cups	water	625 mL
3 tbsp	fresh rosemary leaves	45 mL
1½ cups	granulated sugar	375 mL
2	sprigs fresh rosemary	2

1. Squeeze juice from lemons and set aside. Slice rinds thinly and place in a large stainless steel or enamel saucepan including any seeds and pulp. Add water and bring to a boil over high heat, reduce heat, cover and boil gently for 30 minutes.
2. Add lemon juice and rosemary leaves, return to a boil, cover and boil gently for 10 minutes. Strain through a jelly bag or a strainer lined with cheesecloth.
3. Rinse saucepan and return liquid to pan. Add sugar. Bring to a boil and boil rapidly, uncovered, until mixture will form a gel,★ about 15 minutes, stirring frequently. Remove from heat.
4. Insert a sprig of rosemary into each sterilized jar and ladle jelly into jars. Process as directed on page 16 (Shorter Time Processing Procedure).

Makes 1¾ cups (425 mL).

★ To determine when mixture will form a gel, see page 14.

Peach Amaretto Jelly with Almonds

While in Arizona, Margaret found a beautiful sparkling peach jelly with floating slices of almonds. This is her version.

2 cups	strained peach nectar★	500 mL
¼ cup	strained lemon juice	50 mL
3½ cups	granulated sugar	875 mL
1	pouch (85 mL) liquid fruit pectin	1
2 tbsp	amaretto liqueur	25 mL
¼ cup	sliced almonds	50 mL

1. Combine nectar, lemon juice and sugar in a large stainless steel or enamel saucepan. Bring to a full boil over high heat and boil hard for 1 minute, stirring constantly. Remove from heat and stir in pectin and liqueur.
2. Ladle into sterilized jars. Divide almonds between jars and stir into jelly. Process as directed on page 16 (Shorter Time Processing Procedure).

Makes 4 cups (1 L).

Tip: During processing, you will find that the almonds have floated to the top of the jelly. Stir them into the jelly to redistribute them after opening.

★ Frozen concentrated peach cocktail, which comes in 341 mL cans, may be prepared using 2 parts water rather than 3. Use it to replace peach nectar, reducing sugar to 3 cups (750 mL) because the peach cocktail already contains sugar.

Tropical Fruit Jelly

It's our great fortune to have access to the wonderful exotic flavours of tropical fruits. Passion fruit, mango and papaya combine to give this jelly a truly tropical flavour. Passion fruit juice is worth the effort to find. Look in specialty shops selling Indian and Pacific Rim foods. Be sure to buy the one with no added water.

1½ cups	passion fruit juice	375 mL
½	mango, peeled and cubed	½
½	papaya, peeled, seeded and cubed	½
½ cup	water	125 mL
¼ cup	lime juice	50 mL
1 tsp	grated lime rind	5 mL
3½ cups	granulated sugar	875 mL
1	pouch (85 mL) liquid fruit pectin	1

1. Combine passion fruit juice, mango, papaya and water in a large stainless steel or enamel saucepan. Bring to a boil over high heat, reduce heat, cover and boil gently for 15 minutes. Add lime juice and rind. Remove from heat.
2. Strain juice through a coarse sieve, pressing pulp to extract as much liquid as possible; discard solids. Pour juice through a jelly bag (there should be 2 cups/500 mL—if not, top up with extra passion fruit juice).
3. Combine strained liquid and sugar in saucepan. Bring to a full boil over high heat, stirring constantly. Stir in pectin, return to a full boil and boil hard for 1 minute, stirring constantly. Remove from heat.
4. Ladle into sterilized jars and process as directed on page 16 (Shorter Time Processing Procedure).

Makes 4 cups (1 L).

Red Currant and Raspberry Jelly

The high pectin content of red currants makes them a perfect partner for raspberries, which have much less pectin. The resulting intense red jelly has an exquisite flavour for serving on hot biscuits or muffins. When melted, it makes a wonderful red-hued glaze for a simple fresh fruit tart. This recipe was inspired by a jelly recipe from Fred Yule, one of Margaret's neighbours.

4 cups	red currants, stemmed	1 L
¾ cup	water	175 mL
4 cups	raspberries	1 L
7 cups	granulated sugar	1.75 L
1	pouch (85 mL) liquid fruit pectin	1

1. Using a potato masher, crush currants in a medium stainless steel or enamel saucepan. Add water and bring to a boil over high heat, reduce heat, cover and boil gently for 10 minutes. Add raspberries, return to a boil and boil gently for 3 minutes.
2. Strain mixture through a coarse sieve, pressing pulp to extract juice; discard solids. Pour juice through a jelly bag. You should have a total of 4 cups (1 L) juice.
3. Combine strained juice and sugar in a large stainless steel or enamel saucepan. Bring to a boil over high heat and boil hard for 1 minute, stirring constantly. Remove from heat and stir in pectin.
4. Ladle into sterilized jars and process as directed on page 16 (Shorter Time Processing Procedure).

Makes 8 cups (2 L).

Jalapeño Mint Jelly

Jalapeño peppers and a double hit of mint liven up traditional mint jelly. Try it with crackers and cheese and with lamb or chicken.

1¾ cups	finely chopped fresh mint, divided	425 mL
1½ cups	water	375 mL
3½ cups	granulated sugar	875 mL
¾ cup	cider vinegar	175 mL
2 tbsp	strained fresh lemon juice	25 mL
2	jalapeño peppers, finely chopped	2
1	pouch (85 mL) liquid fruit pectin	1

1. Bring 1½ cups (375 mL) mint and water to a boil in a small saucepan. Remove from heat, cover and let stand for 30 minutes to steep. Strain through a lined sieve pressing with the back of a spoon to extract as much liquid as possible; discard mint.
2. Combine mint liquid, sugar, vinegar, lemon juice and peppers in a large stainless steel or enamel saucepan. Bring to a full boil over high heat and boil hard for 2 minutes, stirring constantly. Remove from heat; stir in pectin and remaining mint.
3. Ladle into sterilized jars and process as directed on page 16 (Shorter Time Processing Procedure).

Makes 4 cups (1 L).

Variation:

Lemon Balm Jelly
Use lemon balm leaves in place of the mint and omit the jalapeño peppers.

Apple Cider Cinnamon Jelly

The full-bodied taste of fresh apple cider spiced with cinnamon is marvellous on toast and hot biscuits. Try heating the jelly and serve over pancakes or French toast. Reserve the cinnamon stick and add a small piece to each jar for an attractive garnish and more intense cinnamon flavour.

2½ cups	fresh-pressed apple cider	625 mL
1	stick cinnamon, 4 inch (10 cm), broken into 4	1
3½ cups	granulated sugar	875 mL
1	pouch (85 mL) liquid fruit pectin	1

1. Combine cider and cinnamon pieces in a large stainless steel or enamel saucepan. Cover and bring to a boil over high heat, reduce heat and boil gently for 5 minutes. Strain cider through several layers of cheesecloth, reserving cinnamon pieces to add to jars. Rinse saucepan.
2. Measure 2 cups (500 mL) cider and return to saucepan; add sugar. Bring to a full boil over high heat, stirring constantly. Stir in pectin, return to a full boil and boil hard for 1 minute, stirring constantly. Remove from heat.
3. Ladle into sterilized jars, add one piece of cinnamon to each jar and process as directed on page 16 (Shorter Time Processing Procedure).

Makes 4 cups (1 L).

White Wine Jelly with Roasted Sweet Peppers

Roasted vegetables are riding a wave of popularity. It isn't hard to understand why once you've tasted this unusual jelly. Use either bottled roasted peppers or Fire-Roasted Pickled Sweet Red Peppers (page 105). We like to serve this jelly with cream cheese on crackers. Or use it as a glaze to brush on chicken as it grills on the barbecue. Wine jellies may take several days to set.

2 cups	dry white wine	500 mL
3 cups	granulated sugar	750 mL
½ cup	roasted red peppers	125 mL
¼ cup	lemon juice	50 mL
1	pouch (85 mL) liquid fruit pectin	1

1. Place wine, sugar, peppers and lemon juice in a large stainless steel or enamel saucepan. Bring to a full boil over high heat and boil hard for 2 minutes, stirring constantly. Remove from heat and stir in pectin.
2. Ladle into sterilized jars and process as directed on page 16 (Shorter Time Processing Procedure).

Makes 4 cups (1 L).

Simple Wine Jelly

This recipe was given to Ellie by her sister-in-law, Jayne, who in turn got it from the host of a bed-and-breakfast. Since the wine is only gently heated and the jelly requires no heat processing, the jelly retains its full wine flavour. It is delicious made from white, red or blush wines and served on hot croissants or biscuits.

Place 1 cup (250 mL) wine and 3 cups (750 mL) granulated sugar in a large stainless steel or enamel saucepan. Bring barely to a boil, making sure sugar is dissolved, stirring constantly. Stir in 1 cup (250 mL) wine and 1 pouch (85 mL) liquid fruit pectin. Ladle into sterilized jars and store in refrigerator. Makes 4 cups (1 L).

Chapter Three

Marvellous Marmalades

M ARMALADES, although similar to jams, always include the pulp of one or more citrus fruits. The citrus rind is suspended in the mixture to intensify the citrus flavour and to add colour and texture. Other fruits are sometimes added to create mouth-watering combinations—for examples, try our Blueberry Orange Marmalade and our Pear Apple Ginger Marmalade (pages 62 and 58).

Since citrus fruits are high in pectin, cooked marmalades require no added pectin to set. The white portion of the rind and the seeds, used in many marmalade recipes, is where most of the pectin is found. They are discarded after cooking if their bitter flavour is not wanted in the finished marmalade. Commercial pectin, however, is needed for our Citrus Freezer Marmalade (page 65) since only the thin outer rind of the citrus fruit is used (it does not contain sufficient pectin to make the gel).

Traditional marmalades get their bittersweet taste from Seville oranges. To many devotees, these are the only true marmalades. Scotch Seville Marmalade (page 55) has a bit of added whisky for a true flavour of Scotland. For a less bitter flavour, try our Apricot Pineapple Marmalade and Microwave Gingered Peach Marmalade (pages 63 and 66); these are both pleasantly sweet.

Serving Suggestions

Use marmalades in sweet bread recipes such as Marmalade Fruit Muffins (page 220) for flavour and moistness. Enjoy Marmalade Sauce (page 217) on waffles or pancakes. Serve Blueberry Orange Marmalade (page 62) to people who are not fond of the more bitter pure citrus ones. A small spoonful of Carrot Marmalade (page 64) is a nice addition to your favourite muffin recipe. Put it on top of each muffin before baking. And most of us adore it on our breakfast toast!

List of Recipes

Scotch Seville Marmalade

The Scots are famous for their marmalades, particularly those made from the bitter Seville orange. Since Seville oranges are only available in late January, this larger recipe makes enough to last through the year. And, of course, it wouldn't be true to Scotland without a dash of Scotch whisky.

4	Seville-type oranges	4
3 tbsp	fresh lemon juice, about 1 lemon	45 mL
5 cups	cold water	1.25 L
⅛ tsp	baking soda	0.5 mL
5½ cups	granulated sugar	1.375 L
1 tbsp	molasses	15 mL
2 tbsp	Scotch whisky, optional	25 mL

1. Squeeze juice from oranges. Reserve seeds and place in a tea ball or tie in a square of cheesecloth. Cut rind into thin shreds. Place orange juice, rind, seeds, lemon juice, water and baking soda in a very large stainless steel or enamel saucepan. Bring to a boil over high heat, reduce heat, cover and boil gently for 1½ hours or until rind is very soft. Stir frequently. Remove and discard seeds.
2. Add sugar and molasses. Bring to a boil and boil rapidly, uncovered, until mixture will form a gel,★ about 15 minutes, stirring frequently. Remove from heat and stir in whisky.
3. Ladle into sterilized jars and process as directed on page 16 (Shorter Time Processing Procedure).

Makes 6 cups (1.5 L).

★ To determine when mixture will form a gel, see page 14.

Fresh Mandarin Orange Marmalade

This delicate, fresh-tasting orange marmalade appeals to those who dislike the intense flavour of traditional marmalades. Clementines, close cousins to the mandarin orange, are often less expensive and just as flavourful. The Fresh Mandarin Orange Cranberry Marmalade (below) makes a festive holiday spread and an attractive gift.

3	mandarin or clementine oranges	3
1	lemon	1
1 cup	water	250 mL
1¾ cups	granulated sugar	425 mL

1. Remove peel from oranges and slice thinly. Place in a small stainless steel or enamel saucepan. Remove thin outer rind from lemon with a vegetable peeler and cut into fine strips with scissors or sharp knife; or use a zester. Add rind and water to saucepan. Bring to a boil over high heat, reduce heat, cover and boil gently for 20 minutes.
2. Remove and discard white rind and seeds from lemon. Chop orange and lemon pulp finely in a food processor or with a sharp knife. Add to saucepan, return to a boil, cover and boil gently for 20 minutes.
3. Add sugar, return to a boil and boil rapidly, uncovered, until mixture will form a gel,★ about 10 minutes, stirring frequently. Remove from heat.
4. Ladle into sterilized jars and process as directed on page 16 (Shorter Time Processing Procedure).

Makes 2 cups (500 mL).

Variation:

Fresh Mandarin Orange Cranberry Marmalade
Add ¼ cup (50 mL) chopped Dried Cranberries (page 195) to marmalade a few minutes before it reaches the gel stage.

★ To determine when mixture will form a gel, see page 14.

Blood Orange Port Marmalade

The intense colours of blood oranges and port wine combine to give this unique marmalade a beautiful deep ruby colour. Use this marmalade as a baste for chicken or fish or invite it to the breakfast table.

2	blood oranges	2
1	lemon	1
1 cup	water	250 mL
½ cup	port wine	125 mL
1¼ cups	granulated sugar	300 mL

1. Remove thin outer rind from oranges with a vegetable peeler and cut into fine strips with scissors or sharp knife; or use a zester. Place in a large stainless steel or enamel saucepan. Squeeze juice from oranges, discarding rind and seeds. Add juice and any pulp to saucepan.
2. Squeeze juice from lemon and slice rind into thin slices. Add lemon juice, rind, water and wine to saucepan. Bring to a boil over high heat, reduce heat, cover and boil gently for 30 minutes.
3. Add sugar, bring to a boil and boil rapidly, uncovered, until mixture will form a gel,★ about 15 minutes, stirring frequently. Remove from heat.
4. Ladle into sterilized jars and process as directed on page 16 (Shorter Time Processing Procedure).

Makes 2 cups (500 mL).

Marmalade Cream
Any marmalade may be used to make this accompaniment for fresh fruit, although Blood Orange Port Marmalade is especially tasty.
Process 1 cup (250 mL) cottage cheese or low-fat ricotta in a blender or food processor until smooth. Remove and stir in ⅓ cup (75 mL) marmalade, 1 tbsp (15 mL) orange liqueur or concentrated orange juice, and 1 square semisweet chocolate, grated. Cover and refrigerate. Serve as a dip or spoon over fresh strawberries, melon, peaches or a fruit of your choice. Makes about 1¼ cups (300 mL).

★ To determine when mixture will form a gel, see page 14.

Pear Apple Ginger Marmalade

This unusual combination of pears and apples produces a very fresh-tasting marmalade.

2	lemons	2
1½ cups	water	375 mL
4 cups	sliced peeled pears	1 L
4 cups	sliced peeled apples	1 L
¼ tsp	baking soda	1 mL
4 cups	granulated sugar	1 L
3 tbsp	finely chopped crystallized ginger (page 196)	45 mL

1. Remove thin outer rind from lemons with a vegetable peeler and cut into fine strips with scissors or a sharp knife; or use a zester. Place in a large stainless steel or enamel saucepan. Remove white rind in large pieces from lemons and place in saucepan. Add water; bring to a boil over high heat, cover, reduce heat and boil gently for 20 minutes.
2. Finely chop lemon pulp in a food processor or with a sharp knife. Add lemon, pears, apples and baking soda to saucepan. Bring to a boil over high heat, cover, reduce heat and boil gently for 20 minutes, stirring frequently. Using tongs, remove and discard the large pieces of rind.
3. Add sugar and ginger to saucepan. Return to a boil over high heat and boil rapidly, uncovered, until mixture will form a gel,★ about 20 minutes, stirring frequently. Remove from heat.
4. Ladle into sterilized jars and process as directed on page 16 (Shorter Time Processing Procedure).

Makes about 5½ cups (1.375 L).

★ To determine when mixture will form a gel, see page 14.

Lemon Marmalade with Vanilla

Those who love the assertive flavour of lemon will particularly enjoy this marmalade. The tartness of the citrus is wonderfully enhanced by the fragrance of fresh vanilla. A splash of tequila makes a spirited variation.

3	lemons	3
1	vanilla bean	1
2 cups	water	500 mL
1½ cups	granulated sugar	375 mL

1. Squeeze juice from lemons; discard seeds. You should have about ⅔ cup (150 mL) juice. Set juice aside.
2. Slice rinds of 2 lemons into very thin slices and place in a large stainless steel or enamel saucepan. Discard rind of third lemon. Split vanilla bean with a sharp knife and carefully scrape soft centre containing the seeds into saucepan. Add bean pod and water. Bring to a boil over high heat, reduce heat, cover and boil gently for 30 minutes.
3. Add juice; return to a boil, cover and boil gently for 10 minutes.
4. Add sugar, bring to a boil and boil rapidly, uncovered, until mixture will form a gel,★ about 15 minutes, stirring frequently. Remove from heat and discard vanilla pod.
5. Ladle into sterilized jars and process as directed on page 16 (Shorter Time Processing Procedure).

Makes 2 cups (500 mL).

Variation:

Margarita Lemon Marmalade
Omit vanilla pod and add 2 tbsp (25 mL) tequila in Step 4 after marmalade is removed from the heat.

Lemon Marmalade Dipping Sauce
Heat 1 cup (250 mL) Lemon Marmalade in a small saucepan until melted. Remove from heat and stir in ¼ cup (50 mL) horseradish. Serve as a dipping sauce with grilled chicken or pork cubes for an appetizer.

★ To determine when mixture will form a gel, see page 14.

Brandied Processor Grapefruit Marmalade

Imagine making a marmalade with no chopping or slicing! Just place all the fruit in a food processor and process. A splash of brandy and you have a gourmet spread that is an ideal gift.

2	small grapefruit (about ½ lb/250 g each)	2
1	lemon	1
2½ cups	water	625 mL
3¾ cups	granulated sugar	925 mL
2 tbsp	brandy	25 mL

1. Cut grapefruit and lemon into large pieces. Remove seeds and place in a tea ball or tie in a square of cheesecloth; set aside. Place fruit in a food processor and pulse until very finely chopped. You should have 2½ cups (625 mL) chopped fruit.
2. Place fruit and seeds in a large stainless steel or enamel saucepan. Add water, bring to a boil over high heat, reduce heat, cover and boil gently for 25 minutes. Remove and discard seeds.
3. Add sugar and bring to a full boil and boil rapidly, uncovered, until mixture will form a gel,★ about 20 minutes, stirring frequently. Remove from heat and stir in brandy.
4. Ladle into sterilized jars and process as directed on page 16 (Shorter Time Processing Procedure).

Makes 4 cups (1 L)

★ To determine when mixture will form a gel, see page 14.

Try the Lemon Marmalade with Vanilla (page 59) on toast or on an English muffin.

Tangerine Grapefruit Marmalade

Tangerines, grapefruit and lemons give this tangy marmalade its unique flavour. As with many marmalades, this one may require several days to set.

2	tangerines	2
2	lemons	2
1	small grapefruit	1
3 cups	water	750 mL
2½ cups	granulated sugar	625 mL

1. Peel tangerines and slice rind thinly. Place rind in a large stainless steel or enamel saucepan. Remove thin outer rind from lemons and grapefruit with a vegetable peeler and cut into fine strips with scissors or sharp knife; or use a zester. Add to saucepan. Remove and discard thick white rind from grapefruit and lemons.

2. Cut all fruit pulp into large pieces and remove all seeds, being careful to catch all juice. Finely chop all fruit pulp in a food processor or blender and reserve. Place seeds in a tea ball or tie in a square of cheesecloth and add to saucepan. Add water, bring to a boil over high heat, reduce heat, cover and boil gently for 20 minutes.

3. Add reserved fruit pulp to saucepan and return to a boil. Cover and boil gently for 20 minutes. Remove and discard seeds.

4. Add sugar to saucepan and return to a boil; boil rapidly, uncovered, until mixture will form a gel,★ about 15 minutes, stirring frequently. Remove from heat.

5. Ladle into sterilized jars and process as directed on page 16 (Shorter Time Processing Procedure).

Makes 3½ cups (875 mL).

★ To determine when mixture will form a gel, see page 14.

For a delicious Jalapeño Mint Jelly, Red Currant and Raspberry Jelly, or an Apple Cider Cinnamon Jelly, turn to pages 49, 50 and 51.

Blueberry Orange Marmalade

Blueberries and citrus enhanced with a hint of cinnamon make this marmalade quite unusual. The recipe is adapted from one developed by the Wild Blueberry Producers Association of Nova Scotia.

1	small orange	1
1	lemon	1
2 cups	water	500 mL
1	cinnamon stick, about	1
	3 inches (7.5 cm) long	
2 cups	fresh or frozen wild blueberries	500 mL
2 cups	granulated sugar	500 mL

1. Squeeze juice from orange and lemon, including any pulp. Discard seeds and set juice aside. Slice rinds into very thin slices. Place rinds, water and cinnamon in a large stainless steel or enamel saucepan. Bring to a boil over high heat, reduce heat, cover and boil gently for 25 minutes or until rinds are very tender. Remove and discard cinnamon stick.
2. Add blueberries and reserved juice; return to a boil, cover and boil gently for 10 minutes.
3. Add sugar; bring to a boil and boil rapidly, uncovered, until mixture will form a gel,★ about 15 minutes, stirring frequently. Remove from heat.
4. Ladle into sterilized jars and process as directed on page 16 (Shorter Time Processing Procedure).

Makes 3 cups (750 mL).

★ To determine when mixture will form a gel, see page 14.

Apricot Pineapple Marmalade

Dried apricots add to the taste and appearance of this easy-to-make marmalade. All the ingredients are available year-round.

½ lb	dried apricots	250 g
1	can (8 oz/250 mL) crushed pineapple with juice	1
1	medium orange, chopped	1
1 cup	granulated sugar	250 mL
¼ cup	chopped maraschino cherries, optional	50 mL

1. Cover apricots with cold water and let stand for 1 hour. Drain and reserve ½ cup (125 mL) liquid. Chop apricots and place in a medium stainless steel or enamel saucepan. Add reserved liquid, pineapple with juice, orange and sugar.
2. Bring mixture to a boil over medium-high heat. Reduce heat and boil gently, uncovered, until mixture will form a gel,★ about 20 minutes, stirring occasionally. Remove from heat and stir in cherries, if using.
3. Ladle into sterilized jars and process as directed on page 16 (Shorter Time Processing Procedure).

Makes 3½ cups (875 mL).

★ To determine when mixture will form a gel, see page 14.

Carrot Marmalade

Who other than the folks at Foodland Ontario would think of using carrots to create a marmalade? Our adaptation calls for quickly chopping carrots and citrus with the aid of a food processor—then simmering them into a delicious marmalade. What a nice way to get some extra beta carotene!

2	medium carrots, peeled	2
1	orange	1
1	lemon	1
1 cup	orange juice	250 mL
1 cup	water	250 mL
3 tbsp	lemon juice	45 mL
3½ cups	granulated sugar	875 mL

1. Finely chop carrots in a food processor or with a knife. You should have 1 cup (250 mL). Place in a large stainless steel or enamel saucepan.
2. Cut orange and lemon into quarters, remove all seeds and chop finely; add to saucepan. Stir in orange juice, water and lemon juice. Bring to a boil over high heat, reduce heat, cover and boil gently for 25 minutes.
3. Add sugar, bring to a boil and boil rapidly, uncovered, until mixture will form a gel,★ about 15 minutes, stirring frequently. Remove from heat.
4. Ladle into sterilized jars and process as directed on page 16 (Shorter Time Processing Procedure).

Makes 4 cups (1 L).

★ To determine when mixture will form a gel, see page 14.

Citrus Freezer Marmalade

Remember this easy recipe anytime you crave the fresh taste of citrus on your breakfast toast.

4 cups	granulated sugar	1 L
¼ cup	very thinly sliced thin outer orange rind (see Tip)	50 mL
2 tbsp	very thinly sliced thin outer lemon rind (see Tip)	25 mL
1½ cups	diced orange pieces (about 3 oranges)	375 mL
¼ cup	diced lemon pieces (about 1 lemon)	50 mL
¼ cup	lemon juice	50 mL
1	pouch (85 mL) liquid fruit pectin	1

1. Place sugar in an ovenproof shallow pan and heat in a 250°F (120°C) oven for 15 minutes to warm sugar. (Warm sugar dissolves better.)
2. Place orange and lemon rind in a small saucepan, cover with cold water, bring to a boil over high heat, reduce heat, cover and boil gently for 15 minutes or until tender; drain.
3. Combine orange and lemon pieces, rind and sugar in a large bowl. Allow to stand for 10 minutes, stirring occasionally.
4. Add lemon juice and pectin; stir constantly for 3 minutes.
5. Ladle marmalade into clean jars or plastic containers to within ½ inch (1 cm) of top rim. Cover with tight-fitting lids. Wipe jars, label and let stand at room temperature until set, up to 24 hours.
6. Store in refrigerator for up to 3 weeks or freeze for longer storage.

Makes 4½ cups (1.125 L).

Tip: Remove the thin outer rind from lemons and oranges with a vegetable peeler and cut into fine strips with scissors or a sharp knife. A handy tool called a zester makes an easy job of removing the coloured outside rind or zest without including the more bitter layer underneath.

Microwave Gingered Peach Marmalade

Ginger adds a peppery pungency to the fresh peach flavour of this delightful marmalade. Freezing peaches in season allows us to make this small-batch microwave marmalade in the winter when oranges and lemons are at their best.

1	medium orange	1
1	lemon	1
½ cup	water or white wine	125 mL
2 cups	finely chopped peeled peaches, fresh or frozen	500 mL
2 cups	granulated sugar	500 mL
2 tbsp	finely chopped crystallized ginger (page 196)	25 mL

1. Remove thin outer rind from orange and lemon with a vegetable peeler and cut into fine strips with scissors or sharp knife; or use a zester. Place rinds and water in a very large microwavable container. Microwave, covered, on High (100%), for 5 minutes, stirring once. Microwave on Medium High (70%) for 5 minutes.
2. Meanwhile, remove and discard white rind and seeds from orange and lemon. Chop orange and lemon pulp finely in a food processor or with a sharp knife. Add to rind mixture. Microwave, covered, on High for 5 minutes, stirring once.
3. Add peaches, sugar and ginger. Microwave, uncovered, on High for 6 minutes, stirring every 3 minutes. Microwave on High for 12 to 15 minutes or until mixture will form a gel,★ stirring every 4 minutes.
4. Ladle into sterilized jars and process as directed on page 16 (Shorter Time Processing Procedure).

Makes 2½ cups (625 mL).

★ To determine when mixture will form a gel, see page 14.

Chapter Four

Conserves,
Butters and Curds

CONSERVES are jams garnished with nuts—walnuts, pecans, almonds—and sometimes with dried fruits. Often more than one fruit is used to give a rich, flavourful spread. Because of this, it generally isn't necessary to add a commercial pectin, since many fruits in combination often produce enough natural pectin to form a light gel.

Fruit butters are made by cooking fruit until it is very soft, and then puréeing it in a blender or food processor. Sugar and often some spices are then added and the mixture cooked until very thick. Traditionally, constant stirring and a heavy-bottom saucepan are required to prevent the butter from burning. Our oven method for Mennonite Oven Apple Butter (page 75), however, is a much easier procedure and gives the same flavourful results.

Fruit butters have that great creamy taste associated with their namesake, butter, but contain no fat. Like butter, they can be used in baking to partially or completely replace the fat. Bran Ginger Muffins and Light Chocolate Brownies (pages 219 and 230) use this increasingly popular lower-fat style of cooking.

Curds, commonplace in grandmother's day, are gaining in popularity as refreshing additions to other foods. The traditional lemon curd was updated with less fat and a far easier microwave method in our first book, *Put a Lid on It!* Newer variations such as Microwave Orange Curd with Candied Peel and Microwave Nectarine Curd (pages 79 and 80) are wonderful variations of this traditional treat.

Serving Suggestions

Serve conserves with a plain cookie and a piece of Brie or Camembert cheese for afternoon tea.

Toast, scones or any hot bread gets a real boost when one of our fruit butters is offered. Since many people do not make their own fruit butters, they make a much appreciated special gift. Wrap the jar in a seasonal fabric, tie with a ribbon and attach the recipe, especially if your gift is going to another cook. Package a jar of fruit butter with a wedge of cheese and a few crackers for an interesting appetizer gift.

Curds are beginning to show up in fashionable restaurants. Fancy bake shops are using them as fillings for meringue shells and spreading them between cake layers. And we love spooning a dollop on waffles for an easy dessert.

List of Recipes

Plum Conserve with Maple Syrup

This conserve is an outstanding example of using both maple syrup and sugar to provide sweetness and a "hint" of maple flavour. Blue plums are best to use in season, but other types may be substituted.

3 cups	chopped, pitted plums (about 1½ lb/750 g)	750 mL
3 cups	chopped, peeled, cored apples (about 3 large)	750 mL
1½ cups	water	375 mL
1	cinnamon stick, 4 inches (10 cm) long	1
2 cups	granulated sugar	500 mL
½ cup	maple syrup	125 mL
	Grated rind of 1 lemon	
1 tbsp	lemon juice	15 mL
¼ cup	chopped hazel nuts	50 mL

1. Combine plums, apples, water and cinnamon in a large stainless steel or enamel saucepan. Bring to a boil over high heat, cover, reduce heat and boil gently for 10 minutes.
2. Add sugar, maple syrup, lemon rind and juice. Return to a boil and boil rapidly, uncovered, until mixture will form a gel,★ about 20 minutes. Remove from heat and stir in nuts.
3. Ladle into sterilized jars and process as directed on page 16 (Shorter Time Processing Procedure).

Makes 5 cups (1.25 L).

★ To determine when mixture will form a gel, see page 14.

Kiwifruit Cranberry Conserve

Tart dried cranberries add a crimson touch to kiwifruit's cool green colour and subtle sweet-tart flavour in this attractive sweet-and-sour conserve.

1¾ cups	finely chopped kiwifruit (about 8 kiwifruits)	425 mL
⅓ cup	water	75 mL
¼ cup	fresh lime juice	50 mL
¼ cup	dried cranberries	50 mL
1¾ cups	granulated sugar	425 mL
¼ cup	toasted pine nuts (see Tip)	50 mL
⅛ tsp	ground nutmeg	0.5 mL

1. Place kiwifruit, water, lime juice and cranberries in a large stainless steel or enamel saucepan. Bring to a boil over high heat, reduce heat, cover and boil gently for 10 minutes or until fruit is tender.
2. Add sugar. Return to a boil, reduce heat and boil gently, uncovered, until mixture will form a light gel,★ about 15 minutes, stirring frequently. Remove from heat.
3. Ladle into sterilized jars and process as directed on page 16 (Shorter Time Processing Procedure).

Makes 2½ cups (625 mL).

Tip: To toast pine nuts, place on a shallow microwavable dish and microwave at Medium (50%) until lightly browned, stirring frequently.

★ To determine when mixture will form a gel, see page 14.

Carrot Raisin Honey Conserve

What a delicious way to eat your carrots! They add interesting colour to the rich taste and texture of raisins and honey. Try it on toast, English muffins or scones.

1	medium orange	1
1	large lemon	1
2 cups	shredded carrots	500 mL
2 cups	water	500 mL
¼ cup	golden raisins	50 mL
2½ cups	granulated sugar	625 mL
1 cup	liquid honey	250 mL
⅓ cup	slivered almonds	75 mL
1 tsp	ground cinnamon	5 mL
½ tsp	ground nutmeg	2 mL
Pinch	ground cardamom	Pinch

1. Cut orange and lemon into quarters, remove seeds and cut each quarter into very thin slices. Combine orange, lemon, carrots, water and raisins in a large stainless steel or enamel saucepan. Bring to a full boil over high heat, reduce heat, cover and boil gently for 20 minutes or until carrots are tender.
2. Stir in sugar and honey. Return to a boil, reduce heat and boil gently, uncovered, until mixture will form a light gel,★ about 15 minutes, stirring frequently. Remove from heat and stir in nuts, cinnamon, nutmeg and cardamom.
3. Ladle into sterilized jars and process as directed on page 16 (Shorter Time Processing Procedure).

Makes about 4 cups (1L).

★ To determine when mixture will form a light gel, see page 14.

Brandied Cranberry Conserve

This spirited conserve with the bright taste of cranberries is adapted from a recipe given to Ellie by her professor at the University of Wisconsin, Dr. Maxine McDivitt, who has made the recipe for years to give as Christmas gifts to faculty and friends.

1	small orange	1
1	cinnamon stick, about 4 inch (10 cm) long	1
3	whole cloves	3
½ cup	water	125 mL
1 tbsp	lemon juice	15 mL
3 cups	cranberries, fresh or frozen (12 oz/340 g pkg)	750 mL
1½ cups	granulated sugar	375 mL
⅓ cup	brandy	75 mL
¼ cup	slivered almonds	50 mL

1. Finely chop orange in a food processor. Combine with cinnamon stick, cloves, water and lemon juice in a medium stainless steel or enamel saucepan. Bring to a boil over medium-high heat, reduce heat, cover and boil gently for 10 minutes. Remove cinnamon and cloves.
2. Add cranberries and sugar. Return to a boil, reduce heat and boil gently, uncovered, until berries pop and mixture will form a light gel,★ about 5 minutes, stirring frequently. Remove from heat and cool slightly; stir in brandy and almonds.
3. Ladle into sterilized jars and process as directed on page 16 (Shorter Time Processing Procedure).

Makes 3½ cups (875 mL).

★ To determine when mixture will form a gel, see page 14.

Festive Peach Conserve with Hazelnuts

The fresh fruitiness of peaches contrasts with the texture and sweet, rich, nutty flavour of hazelnuts in this attractive conserve. Use either fresh or frozen peaches. We often find frozen peaches in bulk food stores or you may choose to freeze your own when fresh peaches are in season.

1	each: lemon, large orange	1
3 cups	finely chopped peeled peaches, fresh or frozen (see Tip)	750 mL
½ cup	water or white wine	125 mL
2½ cups	granulated sugar	625 mL
½ cup	golden raisins	125 mL
¼ cup	chopped candied cherries	50 mL
¼ cup	coarsely chopped hazelnuts	50 mL

1. Remove thin outer rind from orange and lemon with vegetable peeler and cut into fine strips with scissors or sharp knife; or use a zester. Remove and discard remaining white rind and seeds.
2. Finely chop orange and lemon pulp with a knife or in a food processor with on/off motion. Place rinds and pulp in a large stainless steel or enamel saucepan; add peaches and water. Bring to a boil over high heat, boil gently, covered, for 10 minutes or until fruit is tender.
3. Stir in sugar, raisins and cherries. Return to a boil, reduce heat and boil gently, uncovered, until mixture will form a light gel,★ about 25 minutes, stirring occasionally. Remove from heat and stir in hazelnuts.
4. Ladle into sterilized jars and process as directed on page 16 (Shorter Time Processing Procedure).

Makes 3½ cups (875 mL).

Variation:

Festive Nectarine Conserve with Almonds
Replace peaches with same amount of chopped nectarines, and replace hazelnuts with sliced almonds.

Tip: If you freeze your own peaches, it is helpful to measure and label in the amount required for this recipe.

Island Papaya Pineapple Conserve with Rum

This conserve will remind you of a winter holiday somewhere in the tropics. (Usually nuts are added to conserves, but not always—this recipe is an example of the no-nut type.)

1	lime	1
2	papayas, peeled and finely chopped	2
½ cup	crushed pineapple with juice	125 mL
½ cup	water	125 mL
4	whole cloves	4
1	cinnamon stick, broken	1
2½ cups	granulated sugar	625 mL
½ cup	chopped dried apricots	125 mL
2 tbsp	finely chopped crystallized ginger (page 196)	25 mL
1 tbsp	rum	15 mL

1. Remove thin outer rind from lime with a vegetable peeler or zester, chop finely and place in a medium stainless steel or enamel saucepan. Remove and discard remaining white rind from lime; chop lime pulp into small pieces.
2. Add lime pulp, papaya, pineapple, water, cloves and cinnamon stick to saucepan. Bring to a boil over high heat, reduce heat, cover and boil gently for 10 minutes or until fruit is tender. Remove and discard cloves and cinnamon stick.
3. Stir in sugar, apricots and ginger. Return to a boil, reduce heat and boil gently, uncovered, until mixture will form a light gel,★ about 25 minutes. Remove from heat; stir in rum.
4. Ladle into sterilized jars and process as directed on page 16 (Shorter Time Processing Procedure).

Makes 3½ cups (875 mL).

★ To determine when mixture will form a gel, see page 14.

Mennonite Oven Apple Butter

Margaret's neighbour Barbara Cline shares this apple butter recipe with us. It is said to have been brought to Canada by early German settlers. Barbara and her husband own an apple orchard overlooking Georgian Bay, and she prefers to cook the butter in either a slow cooker or the oven. Both methods help to prevent the apple butter from sticking, especially toward the end of the cooking period.

8 cups	peeled, cored and coarsely chopped apples (about 6 large cooking apples)	2 L
1 cup	apple cider	250 mL
2 cups	lightly packed brown sugar	500 mL
½ tsp	ground cinnamon	2 mL
¼ tsp	ground nutmeg	1 mL
⅛ tsp	each: ground allspice and cloves	0.5 mL

1. Combine apples and cider in a shallow baking pan. Bake, covered, in a 400°F (200°C) oven for about 1 hour or until apples are soft; stir once.
2. Remove from oven and purée apples with a hand beater or a food processor until smooth. Return to baking dish, stir in sugar and spices. Reduce oven temperature to 350°F (180°C). Cook apple mixture, uncovered, for about 1 hour, stirring every 20 minutes.
3. Ladle into sterilized jars and process as directed on page 16 (Shorter Time Processing Procedure).

Makes 3 cups (750 mL).

Baker's Prune Butter

Butters are used in many ways. This one is best used as a fat replacement in chocolate cakes and brownies. Its dark colour makes it most suitable for darker-coloured baking.

1¾ cups	boiling water	425 mL
2	tea bags	2
½ lb	pitted prunes	250 g
¼ cup	granulated sugar	50 mL
1 tsp	grated lemon rind	5 mL
½ tsp	vanilla extract	2 mL

1. Pour boiling water over tea bags and steep for 5 minutes; discard bags.
2. Combine tea and prunes in a medium stainless steel or enamel saucepan. Bring to a boil over medium-high heat, reduce heat, cover and boil gently for 5 minutes or until prunes are softened. Remove from heat and purée mixture in a food processor or blender until smooth.
3. Return prune mixture to saucepan, add sugar and lemon rind, and boil gently, uncovered, for 15 minutes or until thickened, stirring occasionally. Remove from heat and stir in vanilla.
4. Ladle into sterilized jars and process as directed on page 16 (Shorter Time Processing Procedure).

Makes about 2 cups (500 mL).

Tip: See page 230 for an excellent low-fat brownie recipe using Baker's Prune Butter.

Cranberry Maple Butter

Use this thick ruby-red preserve as a filling for cakes or over pancakes, fresh fruits or ice cream as well as a fat replacement in muffins (page 219).

1 lb	cranberries (about 5 cups/1.25 L)	500 g
½ cup	apple juice	125 mL
½ cup	pure maple syrup	125 mL
¼ cup	liquid honey	50 mL
½ tsp	ground cinnamon	2 mL
1 tsp	vanilla extract	5 mL

1. Combine cranberries and apple juice in a medium stainless steel or enamel saucepan. Bring to a boil over medium–high heat, reduce heat, cover, and boil gently for 5 minutes or until cranberries pop, stirring frequently.
2. Remove from heat and purée mixture in a food processor until smooth. Press through a sieve and discard seeds. Return sieved mixture to saucepan; add maple syrup, honey and cinnamon and boil gently, uncovered, for 10 minutes or until thickened, stirring occasionally. Remove from heat and stir in vanilla.
3. Ladle into sterilized jars and process as directed on page 16 (Shorter Time Processing Procedure).

Makes 2½ cups (625 mL).

Spiced Squash Butter

What an excellent use for leftover cooked squash! This butter is an excellent fat replacement in muffins or in any other instance where the dark colour of prune butter is inappropriate. And try the carrot variation as a flavourful condiment to serve with salmon, as did a chef at the 1998 Northern Bounty Conference held in Halifax. How much sweet spice you add is up to you. See the tip below using squash butter to thicken gravy.

1½ cups	mashed squash or pumpkin	375 mL
½ cup	apple juice	125 mL
½ cup	lightly packed brown sugar	125 mL
¼ tsp	each: ground cinnamon and nutmeg	1 mL
¼ tsp	vanilla extract	1 mL

1. Combine squash, apple juice, sugar and spices in a medium stainless steel or enamel saucepan. Bring to a boil over medium-high heat, reduce heat and boil gently, uncovered, for about 12 minutes or until mixture is thickened, stirring frequently. Remove from heat and stir in vanilla.
2. Spoon into clean jars or plastic containers, and cover with tight-fitting lids. Refrigerate for up to 1 week or freeze for longer storage.

Makes 1¾ cups (425 mL).

Variation:

Spiced Carrot Butter
Replace mashed squash with same amount of mashed carrot.

Tip: Stir a spoonful of Spiced Squash Butter into the pan juices from roast chicken or pork to produce a wonderful rich-tasting low-fat gravy. Be sure first to remove as much fat as possible from the juices.

Microwave Orange Curd with Candied Peel

Old-fashioned fruit curds are back in style! Adding candied peel to this orange curd makes it utterly mouth-watering. It is wonderful spread on scones warm from the oven. Making any curd in the microwave oven is so much easier and more foolproof than using the traditional double boiler. Just be careful not to over-cook the curd or it will separate.

3	eggs	3
2	medium oranges	2
1	lemon	1
¼ cup	butter	50 mL
¾ cup	granulated sugar	175 mL
⅓ cup	candied orange peel, chopped	75 mL

1. Beat eggs in a 4 cup (1 L) microwavable container.
2. Finely grate thin outer rind from oranges and lemon and reserve. Squeeze juice from oranges and lemon. Measure combined juice to give ¾ cup (175 mL) and whisk into eggs. Add rind, butter and sugar. Microwave, uncovered, on High (100 %) for 2 minutes or until butter is melted and mixture is hot; whisk until smooth.
3. Microwave, uncovered, on Medium (50%) for 2 to 3 minutes or just until thickened, stirring every 30 seconds. (Do not allow it to boil; mixture will thicken as it cools.) Stir in candied peel; let cool.
4. Pour curd into a tightly sealed container. Refrigerate up to 2 weeks or freeze for longer storage.

Makes 2⅓ cups (575 mL).

Variation:

Lime or Tangerine Curd
Replace 2 oranges with 3 limes or 2 tangerines.

Tips:

To get maximum juice from citrus fruit, microwave fruit on High (100%) for 20 seconds before squeezing.
Use Orange Curd as a cake filling, folded into whipped cream to make a light dessert or fill pre-baked tart shells.

Microwave Nectarine Curd

Although curds are traditionally made from citrus fruits, nectarines make a delightful variation. Their delicate flavour, enhanced by a touch of sherry, makes this curd the perfect topping for a fresh fruit cup or a slice of angel food cake.

4	ripe nectarines, halved and pitted (about 1 lb/500 g)	4
¼ cup	water	50 mL
¼ cup	soft butter	50 mL
3	eggs	3
½ cup	granulated sugar	125 mL
2 tbsp	lemon juice	25 mL
1 tbsp	sherry	15 mL

1. Place nectarines and water in a large microwavable container. Cover and microwave on High (100%) for 5 minutes or until boiling. Cool slightly; pull off and discard skins from nectarines. Transfer nectarines and liquid to a food processor or blender, and purée until smooth. Return to container and stir in butter.
2. Beat eggs and sugar until well blended; stir in lemon juice. Whisk into nectarine mixture, mixing well. Microwave, uncovered, at High (100%) for 2 minutes; stir once. Microwave at Medium (50%) for 2 to 3 minutes or just until thickened, stirring every 30 seconds. (Do not allow it to boil; mixture will thicken as it cools.) Stir in sherry; let cool.
3. Pour curd into a tightly sealed container. Refrigerate up to 2 weeks or freeze for longer storage.

Makes 2½ cups (625 mL).

Variation:

Microwave Peach Curd
Replace nectarines with peaches.

Chapter Five

Light 'n' Low Sugar Spreads

S OME people enjoy a less-sweet spread. Others make this choice for dietary reasons. In this chapter we offer six spreads, so-called because they do not have enough sugar to be called a jam.

Since writing *Put a Lid on It!, a* new pectin for making low-sugar spreads (and the one we have used in the three spreads that call for added pectin) has become more widely available. This pectin—Bernardin No Sugar Needed Fruit Pectin—may be used with little or no sugar to make either cooked or uncooked spreads. It is of special interest to those with diabetes or those who prefer low-sugar breakfast spreads since it can also be used with sweeteners such as Splenda or Equal.

Certo has two products: Regular Certo Fruit Pectin Crystals and Certo Light Fruit Pectin Crystals. Regular Certo provides directions for cooked spreads made with no sugar but Certo Light has only directions for uncooked spreads when no sugar is used.

This chapter has three recipes for cooked spreads and three for uncooked spreads. The cooked ones contain no added pectin and achieve their thickness from the natural pectin found in the fruits. They should be processed in a boiling-water canner. The uncooked spreads require added pectin, as do all uncooked spreads. They are stored in the refrigerator for up to three weeks or in the freezer for longer storage. Be aware that spreads made with little or no sugar have a softer set than jams made with sugar.

The following spreads have been analyzed for Canadian Diabetes Association Food Choice Values and Symbols to make them suitable for people with diabetes. Food Choice Values and Symbols and a nutrient analysis are given with each recipe.

Serving Suggestions

Use these spreads as you would any jam.

List of Recipes

Light Gingered Peach Spread

Green apples and ginger add a tart spiciness to peaches in this all-natural fruit spread. Of course, you can always add liquid sweetener to taste before serving, if desired.

2 cups	finely chopped, peeled peaches	500 mL
1	tart green apple, peeled, cored and chopped	1
1 tsp	grated lemon rind	5 mL
½ cup	undiluted frozen apple juice concentrate, thawed	125 mL
2 tbsp	granulated sugar	25 mL
2 tsp	lemon juice	10 mL
¼ tsp	ground ginger	1 mL
⅛ tsp	ground nutmeg	0.5 mL
½ tsp	vanilla extract	2 mL

1. Combine peaches, apple, lemon rind, apple juice, sugar and lemon juice in a medium stainless steel or enamel saucepan. Bring to a boil over high heat, reduce heat and boil gently, uncovered, for 20 minutes or until mixture is thickened and spreadable, stirring frequently.
2. Stir in ginger and nutmeg; simmer for 3 minutes. Remove from heat and add vanilla extract.
3. Ladle into sterilized jars and process as directed on page 16 (Shorter Time Processing Procedure). Once opened, this spread is best kept in the refrigerator and used within 3 weeks.

Makes 3 cups (750 mL).

Each serving: ¹⁄₄₈ of recipe (1 tbsp/15 mL)

1 **++** Extra

Nutritional Information
3 g carbohydrate, 0 g protein, 0 g fat,
0 g fibre, 0 mg sodium, 12 kcal (50 kJ)

Variation:

Light Gingered Pear Spread
Replace chopped peaches with the same amount of chopped pears.

Light Blueberry Pineapple Spread

This all-natural fruit spread uses blueberries in an interesting combination with chopped orange, apple and pineapple juice concentrate, which provides most of the natural sweetness.

1	large orange	1
2 cups	blueberries, fresh or frozen	500 mL
1	tart green apple, peeled, cored	1
½ cup	undiluted frozen pineapple juice concentrate	125 mL
2 tbsp	granulated sugar	25 mL
2 tsp	lemon juice	10 mL
½ tsp	rum extract	2 mL
Pinch	ground nutmeg	Pinch

1. Grate 2 tsp (10 mL) rind from orange; place in a medium stainless steel or enamel saucepan. Remove and discard remaining white rind from orange. Finely chop pulp in a food processor and add to rind.
2. Finely chop blueberries and apple in a food processor. Add to saucepan with pineapple juice, sugar and lemon juice. Bring to a boil over high heat, reduce heat and boil gently, uncovered, for about 25 minutes or until mixture is thickened and spreadable, stirring frequently.
3. Remove from heat and stir in rum extract and nutmeg.
4. Ladle into sterilized jars and process as directed on page 16 (Shorter Time Processing Procedure). Once opened, these spreads are best kept in the refrigerator and used within 3 weeks.

Makes 2 cups (500 mL).

Each serving: ¼₈ of recipe (1 tbsp/15 mL)

1 ++ Extra

Nutritional Information
3 g carbohydrate, 0 g protein, 0 g fat,
0 g fibre, 0 mg sodium, 13 kcal (50 kJ)

Tip: Should extra sweetness be desired, stir in either liquid or granular sweetener to taste before serving.

Light Microwave Cranberry Apple Butter

This spread has the consistency expected of a good fruit butter. The ruby red colour and fresh flavour are excellent served on English muffins and scones.

1½ cups	finely chopped cranberries, fresh or frozen	375 mL
1 cup	finely chopped peeled apple	250 mL
2 tbsp	cranberry juice or water	25 mL
¾ cup	granular low-calorie sweetener with sucralose or aspartame	175 mL
1 tsp	vanilla extract	5 mL
½ tsp	ground cinnamon	2 mL
¼ tsp	ground nutmeg	1 mL

1. Combine cranberries, apple and juice in a 4 cup (1 L) microwavable container. Microwave, uncovered, on High (100%), for 5 minutes, stirring once. Microwave, uncovered, on High for 6 minutes or until mixture is very thick, stirring every 3 minutes.
2. Stir in sweetener, vanilla, cinnamon and nutmeg.
3. Spoon into clean jars or plastic containers to within ½ inch (1 cm) of rim. Cover with tight-fitting lids. Label jars and refrigerate for up to 1 week or freeze for longer storage.

Makes 1⅓ cups (325 mL).

Each serving: ½₀ of recipe (1 tbsp/15 mL)

1 ++ Extra

Nutritional Information
3 g carbohydrate, 0 g protein, 0 g fat,
0 g fibre, 0 mg sodium, 12 kcal (50 kJ)

Tip: This butter may be made into an excellent low-sugar, low-fat breakfast muffin (Bran Ginger Muffins, page 219).

Light No-Cook Raspberry Pineapple Spread

Any fruit-based liqueur makes a nice addition to this fresh-tasting breakfast spread. The spread is excellent with English muffins or scones for afternoon tea.

4 cups	mashed raspberries	1 L
½ cup	pineapple juice	125 mL
1½ cups	water, divided	375 mL
1 cup	granular low-calorie sweetener with sucralose or aspartame	250 mL
2 tbsp	granulated sugar	25 mL
3 tbsp	peach brandy or Cointreau	45 mL
1 tsp	grated orange rind	5 mL
1	box (49 g) "no sugar needed" fruit pectin	1

1. Combine raspberries, pineapple juice, ½ cup (125 mL) water, sweetener, sugar, brandy and orange rind in a large bowl. Let stand for 10 minutes.
2. Gradually stir pectin into remaining water in a small saucepan (do not add pectin all at once). Use wire whisk or fork to mix well. Bring to a full boil over medium-high heat, boil for 1 minute, stirring constantly. Gradually stir into fruit mixture. Let stand for 30 minutes, stirring occasionally.
3. Spoon spread into clean jars or plastic containers to within ½ inch (1 cm) of rim. Cover with tight-fitting lids. Label and refrigerate for up to 1 week or freeze for longer storage.

Makes about 4 cups (1 L).

Each serving: ¼₄ of recipe (1 tbsp/15 mL)

1 ++ Extra

Nutritional Information
2 g carbohydrate, 0 g protein, 0 g fat,
1 g fibre, 0 mg sodium, 12 kcal (50 kJ)

Light No-Cook Strawberry Kiwifruit Spread

Another fresh-tasting freezer spread that uses two very popular and available fresh fruits. Raspberries may be used to replace strawberries for a delectable variation.

3 cups	small ripe strawberries	750 mL
4	kiwifruit, peeled and diced	4
½ cup	pineapple juice	125 mL
1½ cups	water, divided	375 mL
1 tsp	grated lime rind	5 mL
1 tbsp	lime juice	15 mL
1½ cups	granular low-calorie sweetener with sucralose or aspartame	375 mL
2 tbsp	granulated sugar	25 mL
1	box (49 g) "no sugar needed" fruit pectin	1

1. Crush strawberries and kiwifruit in a large bowl; there should be about 3 cups (750 mL). Stir in pineapple juice, ½ cup (125 mL) water, lime rind and juice, sweetener and sugar. Let stand for 10 minutes.
2. Gradually stir pectin into remaining water in a small saucepan (do not add pectin all at once). Use a wire whisk or fork to mix well. Bring to a full boil over medium-high heat. Boil for 1 minute, stirring constantly.
3. Gradually stir into fruit mixture. Let stand for 30 minutes, stirring occasionally.
4. Spoon spread into clean jars or plastic containers to within ½ inch (1 cm) of rim. Cover with tight-fitting lids. Label and refrigerate for up to 1 week or freeze for longer storage.

Makes 3¼ cups (800 mL).

Each serving: ¹⁄₅₂ of recipe (1 tbsp/15 mL)

1 ++ Extra

Nutritional Information
2 g carbohydrate, 0 g protein, 0 g fat,
1 g fibre, 15 mg sodium, 15 kcal (60 kJ)

Light No-Cook Mango Spread

For full-flavoured "touch of the tropics" mango preserves, be sure the mango you choose is slightly soft to the touch. If not, keep it at room temperature for several days and check daily. Mangoes are ripe when they have a fresh, fruity aroma and yield slightly to gentle pressure.

2	large ripe mangoes, peeled and finely chopped	2
1 cup	unsweetened orange juice	250 mL
1 cup	granular low-calorie sweetener with sucralose or aspartame	250 mL
2 tbsp	granulated sugar	25 mL
1 tsp	grated orange rind	5 mL
½ tsp	ground nutmeg	2 mL
1	box (49 g) "no sugar needed" fruit pectin	1
1 cup	water	250 mL

1. Combine mangoes, orange juice, sweetener, sugar, orange rind and nutmeg in a large bowl. Let stand for 10 minutes.
2. Gradually stir pectin into water in a small saucepan (do not add pectin all at once). Use a wire whisk or fork to mix well. Bring to a full boil over medium-high heat. Boil for 1 minute, stirring constantly. Gradually stir into fruit mixture. Let stand for 30 minutes, stirring occasionally.
3. Spoon spread into clean jars or plastic containers to within ½ inch (1 cm) of rim. Cover with tight-fitting lids. Label jars and refrigerate for up to 1 week or freeze for longer storage.

Makes 4½ cups (1.125 L).

Each serving: $\frac{1}{72}$ of recipe (1 tbsp/15 mL)

1 ++ Extra

Nutritional Information
2 g carbohydrate, 0 g protein, 0 g fat,
1 g fibre, 0 mg sodium, 9 kcal (40 kJ)

Condiments
of Choice

Introduction to

Condiments of Choice

PICKLES, relishes, salsas, chutneys, mustards, ketchups—they all add the "spice of life" to our day-to-day meals. These savoury, piquant, salty or spicy accompaniments are an easy way to make an otherwise ordinary meal special.

Condiments are generally made by a pickling process. This process preserves the vegetable or fruit ingredients with an acid, usually vinegar. Good pickling technique is essential to creating great condiments.

Name that Condiment

Pickle is a piece of vegetable or fruit that has been preserved with a salt and/or a vinegar mixture. Pickles may be either sweet or sour and may use herbs or spices to provide extra heat and flavour.

Relish is a pickle that has been chopped rather than left whole. Relishes can be sweet or sour, mild or hot.

Salsa is a Mexican word for "sauce" and can be either cooked or fresh. It has come to refer to a blend of vegetables and/or fruits with spices and herbs.

Chutney is a spicy condiment made from fruit, vinegar, sugar and spices. It originated in India, where it was known by the Hindu word *chatni*. Chutneys can be smooth or chunky and range in spiciness from mild to very hot.

Mustard is a sauce made from seeds of the mustard plant. Its spiciness ranges from mild to hot depending on the method of preparation and the variety of mustard seed. "Prepared" mustards are mustards mixed with other ingredients.

Ketchup is a spicy mixture made from the juice of cooked vegetables and fruits. In North America it is typically made from tomatoes.

Essential Pickling Ingredients

Vegetables and Fruits
Cucumber is the most common vegetable used in condiments. It is essential that cucumbers intended for pickling are not waxed. The thin coat of wax on the skin of the typical smooth green cucumber available in stores throughout the year prevents pickling brine from penetrating the cucumber. English seedless cucumbers are also unsuitable because of their very high water content. The smaller, squatter cucumbers with bumpy skins, sometimes called Kirbys, are the best cucumber for pickling. Remember to remove the blossom end of cucumbers before pickling. It contains enzymes that cause pickles to become soft.

Fruits as well as vegetables make interesting condiments. Whole pickled fruits add a tasty highlight to many meals. Many chutneys, salsas and relishes benefit from a variety of fruit flavours. Do not use frozen fruits or vegetables for making condiments, because freezing softens the texture. This affects the crispness and sometimes the flavour of the condiment. Whether vegetables or fruits are used, the *best* results come from the *best* produce. So choose the freshest and highest quality you can find.

Vinegar
Vinegar is the essential ingredient in the pickling process. It provides the acidity necessary to preserve produce as well as adds a piquant flavour. White vinegar is most commonly used because it does not affect the colour of the condiment. Cider and malt vinegars do affect the colour but are sometimes used for their interesting flavours. All our recipes are based on vinegars that have at least 5% acetic acid. Never use one with less. Check the label for the percentage, and avoid

specialty vinegars as they often are lower in acid. Never reduce the amount of vinegar in a recipe. If you want a product that is less sour, add a bit of sugar instead.

The acid in the vinegar may change the colour of some vegetables. All plant materials contain pigments, some of which are affected by acidity. One change frequently seen is the blue/green colour that develops in garlic in a pickling brine. Don't worry—it is still safe to eat.

Salt

Salt affects both the flavour and texture of the finished condiment. It is important to use only pickling salt. Table salt contains iodine that can turn the condiment dark, as well as anti-caking agents that can give a cloudy appearance.

Sugar and Spice

Sugar is generally added for flavour, but it also helps to keep the preserved condiment firm. Most recipes call for white granulated sugar, but brown sugar and maple syrup may also be added for their flavours.

To maintain clarity of the pickling brine, spices added during cooking should be in their whole form. Either tie them in a small piece of cheesecloth or place them in a large tea ball for easy removal before processing. If you like a stronger spice flavour, add spices to the jar before packing the condiment ingredients. Ground spices are usually added to relishes and chutneys where clarity is not an issue. Always purchase spices in small quantities to keep them fresh, and store them in an airtight container away from heat, light and moisture. A spice rack over the stove may look attractive, but it is not a good place to keep spices fresh!

How To's of Pickling

The first step in pickling is either to sprinkle the vegetables with dry pickling salt or pour a salt brine (salt dissolved in water) over the vegetables. This draws out the moisture, resulting in a firmer product. The choice of method depends on the vegetable and the recipe. Soaking in brine requires more time but we find that generally it is the better method, especially for vegetables cut in pieces. It produces a less salty product than the dry-salt method. With either method, the soaked or sprinkled vegetable must be rinsed and drained to eliminate excess salt.

Preserving foods by pickling relies on exposing the food to an acid in the form of vinegar to discourage bacteria growth. The easiest way to do this is to pour a syrup made of vinegar combined with the salt, sugar or spices specified by the recipe over ingredients already packed into jars.

Condiments must be processed in a boiling-water canner. Grandmother may not have bothered, but it is absolutely essential to ensure the safety of your carefully made condiments. The heat produced by processing destroys the organisms that can grow in high-acid foods and spoil the product. The process also creates an airtight seal that prevents further contamination. The secret to crisp pickles is careful attention to pickling techniques and the right balance of the acid (vinegar) and salt.

Essential Pickling Equipment

Most of the equipment needed for pickling is found in the usual well-equipped kitchen. You need a large stainless steel or enamel *saucepan* for cooking and a *boiling-water canner* and *jar lifter* for processing. Since most condiments are quite thick, a *jar filler or wide-mouth funnel* is very helpful for filling the jars. *Canning jars and lids* of any size can be used, but we like the pint (500 mL) jars for pickles and the half-pint (250 mL) jars for salsas, relishes and chutneys. The very small half-cup (125 mL) jars are ideal for small amounts of savory sauces and for gift giving.

Procedure for Longer Time Boiling-Water Processing

On the following page is the step-by-step procedure for the processing of foods that require 10 minutes or more processing time. Use this procedure for most condiments as directed in the recipes.

Longer Time Processing Procedure

(For food that requires 10 minutes or more processing time.)

If the recipe requires a preparation and cooking time longer than 20 minutes, begin preparation of the ingredients first. Then bring the water and jars in the canner to a boil while the prepared food is cooking. If the ingredients require a shorter preparation and cooking time, begin heating the canner before you start your recipe. The jars do not need to be sterile if the processing time is 10 minutes or longer, but they do need to be hot. Have a kettle with boiling water handy to top up the water level in the canner after you have put in the jars.

Steps for Perfect Processing

20 Minutes Before Processing

Partially fill a boiling-water canner with hot water. Place in the canner a sufficient number of clean mason jars to hold the quantity of food prepared by the recipe. Cover and bring the water to a boil over high heat. This step generally requires 15 to 20 minutes, depending on the size of your canner.

5 Minutes Before Processing

Place snap lids in boiling water 5 minutes before you are ready to fill the jars. Follow the manufacturer's directions.

Filling Jars

Remove jars from the canner and ladle or pack the food into hot jars to within ½ inch (1 cm) of top rim (head space). If the food is in large pieces, remove trapped air bubbles by sliding a clean small wooden or plastic spatula between glass and food; readjust the head space to ½ inch (1 cm). Wipe jar rim to remove any stickiness. Centre snap lid on jar; apply screw band just until fingertip tight.

Processing Jars

1. Place jars in canner and adjust water level to cover jars by 1 inch (2.5 cm). Cover canner and return water to boil. Begin timing when water returns to a boil. Process for the exact time specified in the recipe.
2. Remove jars from canner and cool for 24 hours. Check jar seals (sealed lids turn downward). Remove screw bands, dry and either replace loosely on jar or store separately. Label jars with contents and date and store in a cool, dark place.

Chapter Six

Pickle Perfection

T HE METHOD of pickling can be traced to India, over 4,000 years ago. Today, more than ever, we can revel in the marvellous versatility of pickles. This versatility is reflected in the variety of vegetables—and even a few fruits—in our recipes, including Madras Pickled Eggplant (page 107), which hearkens back to the origins of this condiment.

Did you know that the Japanese serve pickles for dessert? This small piece of trivia "tickled our pickle" imagination. We looked hard and long at the pickles in this chapter and even though pickles are a low-fat choice, we couldn't see any that fit the dessert category.

North Americans are said to eat more than 20 billion pickles each year. While it will no doubt be a long time before the cucumber loses its popularity, we weren't surprised to learn that peppers account for 21% of specialty pickle sales. Fire-Roasted Pickled Sweet Red Peppers (page 105) are one of our favourite specialty pickle recipes since they have so many uses.

Most pickles need a few weeks to mellow before they are ready to eat. For those in a hurry, this chapter contains a recipe for simple overnight pickles, Refrigerator Pickled Melon with Raspberry Vinegar (page 110).

Many foods find their way into a pickle. Cucumbers, cauliflower and beets are favourites, but asparagus, sweet cherries and lemons offer interesting variety.

Here are some techniques for producing the perfect pickle.

- Fresh produce is a must when making a batch of pickled anything.
- Salt vegetables before making them into pickles. This draws out some of the moisture, producing a firmer pickle.
- Cut a thin slice from the blossom end of cucumbers to remove an enzyme that may cause pickles to soften.
- Process pickles in a boiling-water canner to destroy organisms that can cause pickles to soften.
- Check the label on vinegar to make sure that it has at least 5% acetic acid.
- Always use pickling salt.
- Store prepared pickles a few weeks before sampling
- Serve pickles cold and refrigerate pickles after opening.

Serving Suggestions

"Variety is the spice of life" and pickles are a great way to add interest to just about any meal. Pickles are a wonderful accompaniment to richer meats like pork and ham, helping to cut the fat taste. What self-respecting Reuben sandwich would adorn a plate without a kosher dill pickle? Any of our pickles make handy gifts, so make extra jars to have for friends.

List of Recipes

Easy Dilled Pickles

A touch of sugar rounds out the sharp taste often found in traditional versions of this favourite pickle. An overnight stand in a brine assures crispness. Remember to cut away the blossom ends from the cucumbers since they contain an enzyme that can make pickles soft. There is no need to cut the stem ends, but since it is often hard to tell the difference between the two, we like to remove both.

12–16	small pickling cucumbers	12–16
	(about 3 lb/1.5 kg)	
8 cups	water	2 L
¼ cup	pickling salt	50 mL
2 cups	white vinegar	500 mL
2 cups	water	500 mL
1 tbsp	granulated sugar	15 mL
2 tbsp	pickling salt	25 mL
2 tbsp	dried dill seed or 4 large heads fresh dill	15 mL
2 tsp	whole mixed pickling spice	10 mL

1. Cut a thin slice from the ends of each cucumber and place in a non-reactive container. Combine 8 cups (2 L) water and ¼ cup (50 mL) salt, stirring until dissolved. Pour over cucumbers and let stand for 12 hours; drain and rinse under cold water.
2. Combine vinegar, 2 cups (500 mL) water, sugar and 2 tbsp (25 mL) salt in a large stainless steel or enamel saucepan and bring to a boil.
3. Remove hot jars from canner. Divide dill seed and pickling spice equally among jars. Pack cucumbers into jars and pour boiling vinegar mixture over cucumbers to within ½ inch (1 cm) of rim (head space). Process for 10 minutes for pint (500 mL) jars and 15 minutes for quart (1 L) jars as directed on page 93 (Longer Time Processing Procedure).

Makes 4 pint (500 mL) jars.

Cucumber Pickles with Lemon

These pickles will find favour with those who don't like the sharp bite of most pickles. Fresh lemon juice gives a nice lift to the cucumbers.

2 lb	small cucumbers	1 kg
1 tbsp	pickling salt	15 mL
1⅓ cups	white vinegar	325 mL
1 cup	granulated sugar	250 mL
⅔ cup	lemon juice	150 mL
1½ tsp	peppercorns	7 mL
½ tsp	whole allspice	2 mL
3	slices fresh lemon	3
3	cloves garlic	3
3	bay leaves	3

1. Cut a thin slice from the ends of each cucumber and cut into thick slices. You should have about 7 cups (1.75 L). Place in a non-reactive container, sprinkle with salt and let stand for 3 hours; drain. Rinse twice and drain thoroughly.
2. Combine vinegar, sugar, lemon juice, peppercorns and allspice in a large stainless steel or enamel saucepan and bring to a boil over high heat.
3. Meanwhile remove hot jars from canner. Place 1 slice lemon, 1 garlic clove and 1 bay leaf in each pint jar.
4. Add cucumbers to boiling liquid and return just to a boil, stirring constantly. Remove from heat. Remove cucumbers from liquid with a slotted spoon and pack into jars. Pour hot liquid over cucumbers to within ½ inch (1 cm) of rim (head space). Process for 10 minutes for pint (500 mL) jars and 15 minutes for quart (1 L) jars as directed on page 93 (Longer Time Processing Procedure).

Makes 3 pint (500 mL) jars.

Salt-Free Dills with Horseradish

This is the pickle for those who need to reduce their salt intake. Fresh grape leaves are used to produce the crispness traditionally obtained with the use of salt. Either wild or cultivated grape leaves are appropriate.

12–16	small pickling cucumbers (about 3 lb/1.5 kg)	12–16
1	3 x 1 inch (7.5 x 2.5 cm) piece fresh peeled horseradish (see Tip)	1
2½ cups	white vinegar	625 mL
2 cups	water	500 mL
4	fresh grape leaves, washed	4
4	cloves garlic	4
4	heads fresh dill or 4 tsp (20 mL) dill seeds	4
2 tsp	mustard seeds	10 mL

1. Cut a thin slice from the ends of each cucumber. Cut horseradish into 4 lengthwise pieces and reserve.
2. Combine vinegar and water in a saucepan and bring to a boil over high heat.
3. Remove hot jars from canner. Place 1 piece horseradish, 1 grape leaf, 1 garlic clove, 1 head dill and ½ tsp (2 mL) mustard seeds in each jar. Pack cucumbers in jars.
4. Pour boiling vinegar mixture over cucumbers to within ½ inch (1 cm) of rim (head space). Process for 10 minutes for pint (500 mL) jars and 15 minutes for quart (1 L) jars as directed on page 93 (Longer Time Processing Procedure).

Makes 4 pint (500 mL) jars.

Tip: Horseradish adds a bit of flavour, but if you can't find the fresh root, just leave it out.

Pickled Beets and Onions

This pickled beet variation with caraway and mustard seeds adds new interest to a traditional favourite. Use tiny beets and onions for a pickle with a more elegant appearance. But larger ones cut into quarters work just as well.

10–12	small fresh beets	10–12
2 cups	cider vinegar	500 mL
1½ cups	granulated sugar	375 mL
½ cup	water	125 mL
1 cup	peeled small whole onions	250 mL
	(about 4 oz/250 g)	
2 tsp	pickling salt	10 mL
2 tsp	caraway seeds	10 mL
1 tsp	mustard seeds	5 mL

1. Trim beets, leaving 1 inch (2.5 cm) of stem and tap root attached. Place beets in a large saucepan, cover with water and bring to a boil over high heat. Reduce heat, cover and simmer for 25 to 40 minutes or until tender. Drain and rinse under cold water. Remove skins and cut beets into serving-sized pieces if necessary.
2. Combine vinegar, sugar and water in a saucepan. Bring to a boil over high heat, stirring occasionally.
3. Remove hot jars from canner. Divide onions, caraway seeds and mustard seeds equally among jars; add beet pieces.
4. Pour boiling vinegar mixture over beets to within ½ inch (1 cm) of rim (head space). Process for 30 minutes for pint (500 mL) jars and 35 minutes for quart (1 L) jars as directed on page 93 (Longer Time Processing Procedure).

Makes 4 pint (500 mL) jars.

Pickled Ginger

Keep a jar of this easy-to-make pickle on your shelf to make speedy additions to stir-fries. Pickled ginger and its jalapeño and garlic variations also add zest to antipasto plates, meat loaf and any other dishes in need of a pickled spice lift.

1	large piece fresh gingerroot, about 10 oz/280 g	1
¾ cup	rice wine vinegar	175 mL
½ cup	white vinegar	12 mL
2 tsp	soy sauce	10 mL
1 tsp	granulated sugar	5 mL

1. Peel ginger and cut into pieces no larger than 1 inch (2.5 cm). Remove hot jars from canner and pack ginger into jars.
2. Bring vinegars, soy sauce and sugar to a boil in a small saucepan. Pour over ginger to within ½ inch (1 cm) of rim (head space). Process 10 minutes for half-pint (250 mL) and quarter-pint (125 mL) jars as directed on page 93 (Longer Time Processing Procedure).

Makes 2 half-pint (250 mL) jars or 4 quarter-pint (125 mL) jars.

Variations:

Pickled Jalapeños: Replace ginger with 10–12 jalapeño peppers, depending on their size. Omit soy sauce and add ½ tsp (2 mL) salt.

Pickled Garlic: Replace ginger with 3–4 heads garlic, depending on their size. Omit soy sauce and add ½ tsp (2 mL) salt plus 2 tsp (10 mL) pickling spice, if desired.

Tip:

Fresh gingerroot may also be frozen to have on hand to add to a variety of dishes. Freeze it in a tightly sealed freezer bag. When needed, the frozen gingerroot may be easily peeled and grated.

Lemon Spiced Bean Pickle

Green and yellow beans pickled with a bit of lemon are nice with cold meats or on a relish tray. Pack the beans into wide-mouth jars placed on their sides.

1 lb	green beans	500 g
1 lb	yellow beans	500 g
2½ cups	cider vinegar	625 mL
1¼ cups	water	300 mL
1 tbsp	pickling salt	15 mL
1 tbsp	granulated sugar	15 mL
1 tbsp	pickling spice	15 mL
3	strips lemon rind	3

1. Wash and trim beans into 4 inch (10 cm) lengths to fit into jars.
2. Combine vinegar, water, salt and sugar in a medium saucepan and bring to a boil over high heat. Add beans, cover and return to a boil; boil for 1 minute. Remove from heat and drain, reserving liquid. Return liquid to saucepan and bring to a boil.
3. Remove hot jars from canner and place 1 tsp (5 mL) pickling spice and 1 strip lemon rind into each jar. Pack in beans and pour boiling liquid into jars to within ½ inch (1 cm) of rim (head space). Process 10 minutes for pint (500 mL) jars as directed on page 93 (Longer Time Processing Procedure).

Makes 3 pint (500 mL) jars.

Easy Three Bean Salad
A quick salad to serve with barbecued or cold meats.
In a medium bowl, combine 1 cup (250 mL) drained Lemon Spiced Bean Pickle cut into small pieces, ½ cup (125 mL) each: diced celery, drained kidney beans and ¼ cup (50 mL) finely chopped red onion. Bring ½ cup (125 mL) brine drained from pickles, 1 tbsp (15 mL) each sugar and olive oil to a boil. Pour over bean mixture, cover and refrigerate for several hours, stirring occasionally. Makes 2 cups (500 mL).

Pickled Baby Carrots with Oregano and Peppers

Take advantage of packaged tiny peeled carrots to make this easy and interesting pickle. It is adapted from a recipe Janet Jenkinson shared with us. Janet served them at the O'Shea Farm to Canadian home economists attending their 1998 conference in London, Ontario.

3 tbsp	finely chopped fresh oregano or 1 tbsp (15 mL) dried	45 mL
2 tbsp	each: chopped sweet red and green pepper	25 mL
¼ tsp	hot pepper flakes	1 mL
2	small cloves garlic	2
1 lb	peeled baby carrots	454 g
1½ cups	white vinegar	375 mL
½ cup	granulated sugar	125 mL
⅓ cup	water	75 mL
1 tsp	pickling salt	5 mL

1. Combine oregano, peppers and hot pepper flakes. Remove hot jars from canner and divide pepper mixture between them. Add 1 clove garlic to each jar and fill each with half the carrots leaving ½ inch (1 cm) head space. (There may be a few carrots left over.)
2. Meanwhile, combine vinegar, sugar, water and salt in a small saucepan and bring to a boil.
3. Pour hot liquid over carrots to within ½ inch (1 cm) of rim (head space). Process 15 minutes for pint (500 mL) jars as directed on page 93 (Longer Time Processing Procedure).

Makes 2 pint (500 mL) jars.

Mixed Japanese Pickle Sticks

Mirin, a sweet Japanese rice wine, gives these vegetable sticks an interesting flair. This low-alcohol golden wine adds flavour to a variety of Japanese dishes, sauces and glazes. It can be found in any Japanese market as well as the gourmet section of many supermarkets.

4	small zucchini, about 1 lb (500 g)	4
4	medium pickling cucumbers, about 1 lb (500 g)	4
1	piece peeled Japanese white radish (daikon or lobok) (about 1 lb/500 g)	1
2 cups	rice vinegar	500 mL
1 cup	water	250 mL
¼ cup	mirin	50 mL
2 tbsp	pickling salt	25 mL
16	black peppercorns	16
8	whole allspice	8

1. Cut zucchini, cucumbers and radish into lengthwise spears. Set aside.
2. Combine vinegar, water, mirin and salt in a small saucepan and bring to a boil.
3. Remove hot jars from canner. Place 4 peppercorns and 2 allspice in each jar. Pack vegetables into jars. Pour hot vinegar mixture into jars to within ½ inch (1 cm) of rim (head space). Process 10 minutes for pint (500 mL) jars as directed on page 93 (Longer Time Processing Procedure).

Makes 4 pints (500 mL).

Fire-Roasted Pickled Sweet Red Peppers

Roasted red peppers are fast becoming popular for everything from antipasto to pizzas, from garnishing a fresh mozzarella salad to enhancing a robust Italian spaghetti sauce. This recipe, adapted from one developed by Bernardin Canada, lets you roast peppers in the summer when they are plentiful to enjoy during the winter months.

6–8	small sweet red peppers (about 2 lb/900 g)	6–8
1	large clove garlic, unpeeled	1
½ cup	dry white wine	125 mL
½ cup	white vinegar	125 mL
¼ cup	cider vinegar	50 mL
½ cup	coarsely chopped onion	125 mL
2 tbsp	granulated sugar	25 mL
½ tbsp	dried oregano leaves or 1 tbsp (15 mL) fresh	7 mL
1 tsp	pickling salt	5 mL

1. Roast peppers and garlic on the barbecue grill or on a rack under the broiler until skins are blistered and starting to blacken. Place peppers in a paper bag until cool enough to handle; set garlic aside. When peppers are cool, remove skins, cores and seeds. Cut lengthwise into strips about 1 inch (2.5 cm) wide; set aside.
2. Combine wine, vinegars, onion, sugar, oregano and salt in a small stainless steel or enamel saucepan. Squeeze roasted garlic to remove from skin, mash and add to saucepan. Bring mixture to a boil over high heat, reduce heat and boil gently for 5 minutes.
3. Remove hot jars from canner and pack peppers into jars to within ¾ inch (2 cm) of top rim, being careful not to pack too tightly. Pour boiling vinegar mixture including onions to within ½ inch (1 cm) of rim (head space). Process 15 minutes for half-pint (250 mL) and pint (500 mL) jars as directed on page 93 (Longer Time Processing Procedure).

Makes 4 half-pint (250 mL) jars.

Herbed Asparagus Pickles

Tarragon appears in the spring just as asparagus begins to push out of the ground. The two combine to make a savoury pickle that is quite out-of-the-ordinary.

2½–3 lb	asparagus spears	1.2–1.5 kg
4	sprigs fresh tarragon	4
2	small dry shallots, halved	2
2 cups	white wine vinegar	500 mL
1½ cups	white vinegar	375 mL
1 cup	water	250 mL
¼ cup	granulated sugar	50 mL
1 tsp	pickling salt	5 mL

1. Wash asparagus and cut each spear 4¼ inches (11 cm) long or long enough to fit a wide-mouth pint (500 mL) jar leaving ¾ inch (2 cm) head space.
2. Remove hot jars from canner and pack asparagus into jars with tips down. Tuck a sprig of tarragon and half a shallot among the spears.
3. Meanwhile, combine wine vinegar, white vinegar, water, sugar and salt in a medium saucepan and bring to a boil. Pour boiling vinegar mixture over asparagus to within ½ inch (1 cm) of rim (head space). Process 15 minutes for pint (500 mL) jars as directed on page 93 (Longer Time Processing Procedure).

Makes 4 pint (500 mL) jars.

Madras Pickled Eggplant

Yvonne LeFebour, a friend of Margaret's daughter Martha, brought this wonderful family recipe with her from Calicut, India, when she came to live in Canada. It has unique Indian flavours that are quite delightful. Our only change has been to reduce the amount of oil. The heat level can be controlled to suit your own taste buds (see Tip).

2 lb	eggplant (2 large)	1 kg
3 tbsp	white vinegar	45 mL
2	large cloves garlic, minced	2
2 tbsp	chile powder	25 mL
2 tsp	each: ground ginger and turmeric	10 mL
⅓ cup	canola oil	75 mL
1 tbsp	each: cumin seeds and fenugreek seeds	15 mL
1¼ cups	white vinegar	300 mL
1 cup	granulated sugar	250 mL
2–4	finely chopped and seeded small hot red chiles or jalapeño peppers	2–4
¼ cup	finely chopped gingerroot	50 mL
2 tbsp	pickling salt	25 mL

1. Cube unpeeled eggplant into bite-sized pieces and reserve.
2. Combine 3 tbsp (45 mL) vinegar, garlic, chile powder, ginger and turmeric in a small bowl to form a paste and reserve.
3. Heat oil on medium-high heat in a large saucepan. Add cumin and fenugreek seeds and sauté for 1 minute. Add eggplant and sauté for about 10 minutes or until eggplant is just tender. Reduce heat and add reserved paste and 1¼ cups (300 mL) vinegar, sugar, chile: peppers, gingerroot and salt. Stir over medium heat for about 5 minutes or until boiling.
4. Remove hot jars from canner and ladle pickles into jars to within ½ inch (1 cm) of rim (head space). Process for 15 minutes for half-pint (250 mL) jars and 20 minutes for pint (500 mL) jars as directed on page 93 (Longer Time Processing Procedure).

Makes 3 pint (500 mL) jars.

Tip: Whether to use milder jalapeño peppers or 2–4 of the smaller and hotter red chile peppers depends on the heat level you enjoy.

Pickled Sweet Cherries

This unusual and colourful pickle with its sweet-sour taste makes an excellent condiment for game and poultry as well as other roasted meats.

1¾ cups	white vinegar	425 mL
1¾ cups	granulated sugar	425 mL
¾ cup	water	175 mL
2	cinnamon sticks, about 4 inches (10 cm) long	2
2 tsp	whole cloves	10 mL
1 tsp	whole allspice	5 mL
2 lb	dark sweet cherries with stems	1 kg

1. Combine vinegar, sugar, water, cinnamon, cloves and allspice in a small saucepan. Bring to a boil, reduce heat and boil gently, uncovered, for 20 minutes.
2. Remove hot jars from canner and pack cherries into jars. Pour hot syrup over cherries to within ½ inch (1 cm) of rim (head space). Process 10 minutes for pint (500 mL) jars as directed on page 93 (Longer Time Processing Procedure).

Makes 3 pint (500 mL) jars.

Spiced Lemon Slices

These interesting pickled lemon slices make a lovely and different garnish for a fish entrée. They are also an attractive and unusual addition to a condiment tray.

4	large lemons	4
8 cups	hot water	2 L
1 tsp	pickling salt	5 mL
1 cup	granulated sugar	250 mL
½ cup	lightly packed brown sugar	125 mL
½ cup	each: cider vinegar and water	125 mL
¼ cup	corn syrup	50 mL
6	whole cloves	6
3	cardamom pods	3
3	cinnamon sticks, 3 inches (7.5 cm) long	3
½ tsp	peppercorns	2 mL

1. Combine whole unpeeled lemons, 8 cups (2 L) hot water and salt in a large saucepan. Bring to a boil, reduce heat, cover and simmer for 20 minutes or until fruit is tender. Drain lemons, discarding liquid, and cool.
2. Cut lemons in half and then into paper-thin slices.
3. Combine granulated sugar, brown sugar, vinegar, water, corn syrup and spices in a large saucepan. Stir over high heat until sugars have dissolved. Reduce heat and cook, uncovered, for 10 minutes. Add lemon slices, cover and cook gently for 15 minutes. Remove from heat and let stand for 5 minutes.
4. Remove hot jars from canner. Remove lemon slices from liquid with a slotted spoon; pack into jars. Pour liquid and spices over lemons to within ½ inch (1 cm) of top rim (head space). Process for 10 minutes for half-pint (250 mL) jars as directed on page 93 (Longer Time Processing Procedure).

Makes 3 half-pint (250 mL) jars.

Spiced Lemon–Slice Salad
Drain liquid from Spiced Lemon Slices and blend liquid with ⅓ cup (75 mL) mayonnaise and ½ tsp (2 mL) curry powder. Just before serving, pour dressing over a salad of shredded romaine lettuce and finely chopped red onion. Add lemon slices and toss.

Refrigerator Pickled Melon with Raspberry Vinegar

Three varieties of melon and raspberry vinegar make this a very different pickle. Crunchy, attractive and perfectly delicious, these easy-to-make refrigerator pickles are bound to become popular at your house. They are especially good with cold chicken, turkey, pork or ham.

2 cups	cubed cantaloupe	500 mL
2 cups	honeydew melon	500 mL
1 cup	cubed watermelon	250 mL
¼ cup	Red Wine Raspberry Vinegar (page 181)	50 mL
1 tbsp	lemon juice	15 mL
2 tsp	granulated sugar	10 mL
½ tsp	salt	2 mL
	Chopped fresh mint leaves	

1. Combine cantaloupe, honeydew and watermelon in a medium bowl.
2. Stir together vinegar, lemon juice, sugar and salt. Pour over fruit, cover and refrigerate for several hours before serving. Sprinkle with chopped mint and spoon into a glass serving dish. Keep up to three days in refrigerator.

Makes about 5 cups (1.25 L).

Freezer Bread and Butter Pickles

A fast variation of a traditional favourite, this easy recipe requires little preparation and no processing time. Either English or small pickling cucumbers can be used.

4 cups	thinly sliced cucumbers	1 L
	(about ³⁄₁₆ inch/4 mm thick)	
1 cup	thinly sliced onion	250 mL
1	sweet red pepper, thinly sliced	1
2 tsp	pickling salt	10 mL
1½ cups	cider vinegar	375 mL
⅔ cup	granulated sugar	150 mL
1 tsp	mustard seeds	5 mL
½ tsp	celery seeds	2 mL
½ tsp	turmeric	2 mL

1. Place cucumbers, onion and red pepper in a large non–reactive container. Sprinkle with salt and mix well. Let stand for 3 hours, stirring occasionally. Rinse twice and drain thoroughly.
2. Heat vinegar in microwave oven for 30 seconds or warm slightly on the stove top. Combine vinegar, sugar, mustard seeds, celery seeds and turmeric in a small bowl stirring until sugar is dissolved. Pour over vegetables and mix well.
3. Pack vegetables into small freezer containers. Divide liquid and pour over pickles. Seal tightly and freeze.
4. Store pickles in freezer up to 6 months. Once thawed, use them within several days before they lose their crunch.

Makes about 3 cups (750 mL).

Chapter Seven

Ravishing Relishes

R ELISHES may only be chopped pickles, but they enjoy a multi-
tude of uses. From simple hot dogs with Barbecue Relish (page
115) to an elegant lamb dinner graced with Processor Apple
Mint Relish (page 122), relishes hold their own with their pickle cousins.

Relishes have been around for so long that many have interesting histories.
One of these is the chow chow relish. It is thought by some to have been created
for Europeans residing in China. Another story has it that the chef to Napoleon
developed the original chow chow relish and yet another that Chinese railroad
labourers brought it to America. Whatever the origin, chow chow is a popular
relish and we trust our Cauliflower Chow Chow (page 118) will win your heart.

Relishes are made from many different fruits and vegetables with many added
herbs and spices. It is best to chop the ingredients in about the same sized pieces
so they have similar cooking times. And like pickles, relishes should be processed
in a boiling-water canner.

Serving Suggestions

Many great creamy salad dressings benefit from a spoonful of relish. Potato salad is
also much tastier with a dollop of Sun Relish (page 116) stirred in. Look for the
Caramelized Red Onion and Tomato Pizza on page 214 and Zucchini Corn Salad
made with Fiesta Corn Relish (page 117). Did you ever consider adding some relish to a meat loaf? You may never again make one without! Try it with hamburger

patties, too. And of course, there is that combination of mustard and relish that turns the lowly hot dog and hamburger into gustatory delights.

List of Recipes

Easy Oven Relish

A fruity oven-prepared relish makes a delicious accompaniment to cold meats, meat loaves and roasts, and goes well with sandwiches. See page 227 for Garden Pasta Salad with this relish used as a dressing.

3	large peaches, peeled, pitted and coarsely chopped	3
3	pears, peeled, cored and coarsely chopped	3
1	can (28 oz/798 mL) tomatoes or 4 large tomatoes, peeled and chopped	1
2	large onions, finely chopped	2
1	large sweet green pepper, chopped	1
1	stalk celery, finely chopped	1
1½ cups	granulated sugar	375 mL
1½ cups	cider vinegar	375 mL
1 tbsp	whole allspice (tied in cheesecloth)	15 mL
1 tbsp	pickling salt	15 mL

1. Combine peaches, pears, tomatoes, onions, green pepper, celery, sugar, vinegar, allspice and salt in a large metal roasting pan.
2. Bring to a boil over medium heat, stirring occasionally. Transfer roasting pan to a 375°F (190°C) oven and bake, uncovered, for about 1½ hours or until mixture is thickened; stir occasionally. Remove from oven and discard allspice bag.
3. Remove hot jars from canner and ladle relish into jars to within ½ inch (1 cm) of rim (head space). Process for 10 minutes for half-pint (250 mL) jars and 15 minutes for pint (500 mL) jars as directed on page 93 (Longer Time Processing Procedure).

Makes 5 cups (1.25 L).

Easy Seafood Sauce
Stir 2 tbsp (25 mL) ketchup, 1 tbsp (15 mL) horseradish and a splash of lemon juice into ½ cup (125 mL) of the Easy Oven Relish.

Barbecue Relish

A recipe from Judi Kingry of Bernardin Canada was the inspiration for this easy-to-make relish—so right with everything from hot dogs and hamburgers to egg salad or cold meat sandwiches.

4 cups	finely chopped zucchini (about 2 large)	1 L
1 cup	finely chopped onion	250 mL
1	medium sweet red, green or yellow pepper, finely chopped	1
½ cup	finely chopped celery	125 mL
2 tbsp	pickling salt	25 mL
1½ cups	granulated sugar	375 mL
1¼ cups	white vinegar (see Tip)	300 mL
1 tbsp	celery seed, optional	15 mL
1 tsp	mustard seed	5 mL
½ tsp	each: dry mustard and ground cloves	2 mL

1. Combine zucchini, onion, pepper and celery in a large non-reactive bowl. Sprinkle with salt and cover with cold water; let stand for 1 hour. Drain vegetables in a sieve, pressing out excess moisture; reserve vegetables.
2. Combine sugar, vinegar, celery seed (if using), mustard seed, dry mustard and cloves in a large stainless steel or enamel saucepan. Bring to a boil over high heat; add reserved vegetable mixture. Return to a boil, reduce heat and boil gently, uncovered, for 45 minutes or until mixture is thickened.
3. Remove hot jars from canner and ladle relish into jars to within ½ inch (1 cm) of rim (head space). Process for 10 minutes for half-pint (250 mL) jars and 15 minutes for pint (500 mL) jars as directed on page 93 (Longer Time Processing Procedure).

Makes 3¼ cups (800 mL).

Tip: Replace one half of the white vinegar with cider vinegar for a change of taste.

Sun Relish

Combining peaches and yellow peppers gives this relish its sweet and hot flavours and its "sunny" colour. It is an inspired addition to cream cheese or to a wedge of Canadian cheddar. While best with cheeses, it also goes well with warm biscuits and omelets.

6	peaches, peeled, pitted and chopped	6
6	sweet yellow peppers, seeded and chopped	6
1	hot yellow pepper, seeded and chopped	1
1	lemon, halved	1
½ cup	white wine vinegar	125 mL
2½ cups	granulated sugar	625 mL
1½ tsp	pickling salt	7 mL

1. Place peaches, peppers, lemon and vinegar in a large stainless steel or enamel saucepan. Bring to a boil over medium–high heat, reduce heat and boil gently, uncovered, for 30 minutes or until softened. Remove and discard lemon, add sugar and salt; return to a boil. Cook, uncovered, for about 20 minutes or until mixture thickens, stirring frequently.
2. Remove hot jars from canner and ladle relish into jars to within ½ inch (1 cm) of rim (head space). Process for 10 minutes for half-pint (250 mL) jars and 15 minutes for pint (500 mL) jars as directed on page 93 (Longer Time Processing Procedure).

Makes 4 cups (1 L).

Fiesta Corn Relish

We especially like serving this colourful relish with cold meats and barbecued burgers. There is a hint of the Southwest in its flavours and its bit of heat. Frozen corn is almost as delicious as fresh corn, so this relish can be made any time of year.

5–6	large ears fresh corn (see Tip)	5–6
1	hot yellow pepper, seeded and finely chopped	1
2	cloves garlic, minced	2
1½ cups	cider vinegar	375 mL
¾ cup	granulated sugar	175 mL
½ cup	chopped red onion	125 mL
½ cup	chopped sweet red pepper	125 mL
⅓ cup	chopped green onions	75 mL
1 tsp	ground cumin	5 mL
1 tsp	pickling salt	5 mL
½ tsp	freshly ground black pepper	2 mL
2 tbsp	chopped fresh cilantro	25 mL

1. Bring a large pot of water to a boil over high heat. Add corn, cover and cook for 6 minutes. Drain and cool until easy to handle. With a sharp knife cut kernels from cob and measure 4 cups (1 L) corn into a large stainless steel or enamel saucepan.
2. Add hot pepper, garlic, vinegar, sugar, onion, red pepper, green onions, cumin, salt and black pepper to saucepan. Bring to a boil over high heat, reduce heat and boil gently, uncovered, for 20 minutes. Stir in cilantro and cook 2 minutes longer. Remove from heat.
3. Remove hot jars from canner and ladle relish into jars to within ½ inch (1 cm) of rim (head space). Process 15 minutes for half-pint (250 mL) jars and pint (500 mL) jars as directed on page 93 (Longer Time Processing Procedure).

Makes 4½ cups (1.125 L).

Tip: To make this relish when fresh corn is unavailable, you can use 4 cups (1 L) frozen corn.

Cauliflower Chow Chow

Originally chow chow was a Chinese condiment made from ginger, fruits and peels preserved in a heavy syrup. More recently, it has come to refer to a relish of mixed vegetables in a mustard sauce. In Canada, it is often given such names as Lady Ross or Lady Ashburnham.

3 cups	cauliflower florets, coarsely chopped (about ½ head)	750 mL
2	small pickling cucumbers, peeled and chopped	2
1	sweet green pepper, seeded and chopped	1
1	small hot red chile pepper, seeded and chopped	1
1	onion, chopped	1
3 tbsp	pickling salt	45 mL
3 cups	lukewarm water	750 mL
⅔ cup	granulated sugar	150 mL
3 tbsp	all-purpose flour	45 mL
2 tsp	each: dry mustard and celery seeds	10 mL
½ tsp	each: curry powder and turmeric	2 mL
⅔ cup	each: cider vinegar and white vinegar	150 mL
⅓ cup	water	75 mL

1. Toss together cauliflower, cucumbers, green pepper, chile pepper and onion in a large non-reactive bowl. Stir salt and lukewarm water together and pour over vegetables. Let stand for 8 to 10 hours. Drain vegetables in a sieve; rinse twice and drain thoroughly.
2. Combine sugar, flour, mustard, celery seeds, curry powder and turmeric in a large stainless steel or enamel saucepan. Add vinegars and water, stirring to blend well. Bring to a boil over high heat, stirring constantly until mixture thickens. Add the drained vegetables, return to a boil, reduce heat and boil gently, uncovered, for 10 minutes.
3. Remove hot jars from canner and ladle relish into jars to within ½ inch (1 cm) of rim (head space). Process 10 minutes for half-pint (250 mL) jars and pint (500 mL) jars as directed on page 93 (Longer Time Processing Procedure).

Makes 3½ cups (875 mL).

Caponata

Caponata is a Sicilian dish served as a salad, side dish or relish. We also like it as an appetizer spread on toasted baguette slices.

1	small eggplant, cut into ½ inch (1 cm) cubes	1
1 ½ tbsp	pickling salt	20 mL
2	large tomatoes, peeled and chopped	2
1	medium sweet red pepper, diced	1
1 cup	diced zucchini	250 mL
½ cup	chopped onion	125 mL
3	large cloves garlic, chopped	3
¼ cup	chopped stuffed olives	50 mL
1 tbsp	capers, rinsed	15 mL
1	bay leaf	1
1 tsp	fresh thyme or ¼ tsp (1 mL) dried	5 mL
¼ tsp	each: salt and freshly ground pepper	1 mL
⅓ cup	red wine vinegar	75 mL
2 tsp	each: granulated sugar and olive oil	10 mL
2 tbsp	tomato paste	25 mL

1. Place eggplant in a non-reactive bowl. Sprinkle with salt and stir well. Let stand for 2 hours. Drain eggplant in a sieve and rinse twice, draining thoroughly; press out excess moisture.
2. Place eggplant, tomatoes, red pepper, zucchini, onion, garlic, olives, capers, bay leaf, thyme, salt and pepper in a large roasting pan.
3. Heat vinegar, sugar and oil in a microwavable container until hot, about 1 minute; stir into vegetables. Bake in a 350°F (180°C) oven for about 1½ hours (1 hour for a convection oven), or until vegetables are softened and liquid has evaporated, stirring every 20 minutes. Remove pan from oven, discard bay leaf and stir in tomato paste.
4. Remove hot jars from canner and spoon relish into jars to within ½ inch (1 cm) of rim (head space). Process for 15 minutes for half-pint (250 mL) jars and 20 minutes for pint (500 mL) jars as directed on page 93 (Longer Time Processing Procedure).

Makes 5 cups (1.25 L

Cranberry Apple Pear Relish

The combination of apples and pears gives this versatile relish a lovely freshness as well as extending the cranberries. Orange liqueur and juice add a citrus flavour. We like using this relish with poultry or as an appetizer with crackers and cheddar cheese.

1	pkg (340 g) fresh or frozen cranberries	1
3	apples, peeled, cored and diced	3
2	pears, peeled, cored and diced	2
1½ cups	golden raisins	375 mL
2 cups	granulated sugar	500 mL
1 cup	orange juice	250 mL
2 tbsp	grated orange rind	25 mL
2 tsp	ground cinnamon	10 mL
¼ tsp	ground nutmeg	1 mL
½ cup	orange liqueur	125 mL

1. Combine cranberries, apples, pears, raisins, sugar, orange juice and rind, cinnamon and nutmeg in a large stainless steel or enamel saucepan. Bring to a boil over high heat, stirring frequently. Reduce heat and boil gently, uncovered, for about 25 minutes or until mixture thickens, stirring occasionally. Remove from heat and stir in liqueur.
2. Remove hot jars from canner and ladle relish into jars to within ½ inch (1 cm) of rim (head space). Process for 10 minutes for half pint (250 mL) jars and 15 minutes for pint (500 mL) jars as directed on page 93 (Longer Time Processing Procedure).

Makes 6 cups (1.5 L).

Oven-Baked Carrots
This vegetable casserole using Cranberry Apple Pear Relish makes a tasty accompaniment for roasted meats.
Coarsely grate 6 carrots and place in a lightly greased 6 cup (1.5 L) casserole. Stir in ¾ cup (175 mL) Cranberry Apple Pear Relish; dot with 1 tbsp (15 mL) butter or margarine. Add 2 tbsp (25 mL) water, cover and bake in a 325°F (160°C) oven for 45 minutes. Uncover and continue to bake 10 minutes longer or until carrots are tender. Makes 6–8 servings.

Caramelized Red Onion Relish

Balsamic vinegar is the magic ingredient in this recipe. It adds a pungent sweetness to the caramelized onions. Serve with barbecued or broiled meats such as steak, lamb chops and chicken. See page 214 for an easy appetizer pizza using this spread.

2	large red onions, peeled	2
¼ cup	firmly packed brown sugar	50 mL
1 cup	dry red wine	250 mL
3 tbsp	balsamic vinegar	45 mL
Pinch	each: salt and freshly ground pepper	Pinch

1. Slice onions into very thin slices. Combine onions and sugar in a heavy non-stick skillet. Cook, uncovered, over medium-high heat for about 25 minutes or until onions turn golden and start to caramelize, stirring frequently.
2. Stir in wine and vinegar. Bring to a boil over high heat, reduce heat to low and cook for about 15 minutes or until most of the liquid has evaporated, stirring frequently.
3. Season to taste with salt and pepper. Spoon into a clean wide-mouthed jar and cool briefly.
4. Remove hot jars from canner and ladle relish into jars to within ½ inch (1 cm) of rim (head space). Process for 10 minutes for half-pint (250 mL) jars as directed on page 93 (Longer Time Processing Procedure).

Makes 2 cups (500 mL).

Tip: This small-batch recipe probably won't last long enough to bother processing in a hot-water bath. If you follow these instructions, you may refrigerate it for up to 3 weeks or even freeze for longer storage.

Processor Apple Mint Relish

Fresh mint, apples and a hint of ginger combine to make this unique and refreshing relish. It is quick to make in a food processor. While the relish enhances most foods, we especially like it with fish, lamb and grilled chicken.

4	medium tomatoes, peeled	4
2	large tart apples, peeled and cored	2
1	large onion	1
½	sweet green pepper	½
1¼ cups	white vinegar	300 mL
2 tsp	grated gingerroot	10 mL
1 tsp	mustard seeds	5 mL
1 cup	fresh mint leaves, tightly packed	250 mL
¾ cup	granulated sugar	175 mL
¼ tsp	pickling salt	1 mL

1. Coarsely chop tomatoes, apples, onion and pepper in small batches in a food processor or by hand. Transfer to a large stainless steel or enamel saucepan; add vinegar, gingerroot and mustard seeds. Bring to a boil over high heat, reduce heat, cover and boil gently for 20 minutes or until mixture is soft.
2. Meanwhile, chop mint in a food processor or by hand. Stir mint, sugar and salt into saucepan, return to a boil and boil gently, uncovered, for 10 minutes or until most of liquid has evaporated, stirring occasionally. (Relish will thicken on cooling.)
3. Remove hot jars from canner and ladle relish into jars to within ½ inch (1 cm) of rim (head space). Process 10 minutes for half-pint (250 mL) jars and pint (500 mL) jars as directed on page 93 (Longer Time Processing Procedure).

Makes 5 cups (1.25 L).

Indian-Style Cucumber Relish

Seasoned with traditional spices, cumin, and black and yellow mustard seeds, this relish shows its East Indian heritage. Use it to pep up meats or poultry. Mixed with yogurt it becomes raita, a salad that is served with Indian food as a cool counterpoint to spicy dishes.

6 cups	diced peeled cucumber	1.5 L
	(about 8–12 medium pickling cucumbers)	
2 cups	thinly sliced onions	500 mL
1 tbsp	pickling salt	15 mL
2 cups	white vinegar	500 mL
½ cup	granulated sugar	125 mL
1 tbsp	whole cumin seeds	15 mL
2 tsp	black mustard seeds	10 mL
2 tsp	yellow mustard seeds	10 mL

1. Place cucumber and onion in a non-reactive bowl and sprinkle with salt. Let stand for 4 hours, stirring occasionally. Drain vegetables in a sieve, rinse twice and drain thoroughly.
2. Combine vinegar, sugar, cumin seeds and mustard seeds in a large stainless steel or enamel saucepan. Bring to a boil over high heat. Add vegetables and return to a boil for 30 seconds.
3. Remove hot jars from canner. Remove vegetables from liquid with a slotted spoon; pack into jars. Pour liquid over cucumber to within ½ inch (1 cm) of rim (head space). Process 10 minutes for pint (500 mL) jars as directed on page 93 (Longer Time Processing Procedure).

Makes 3 pint (500 mL) jars.

Cucumber Raita
Drain and discard liquid from 1 pint (500 mL) jar Indian-Style Cucumber Relish. Place relish in a serving bowl. Stir in ¾ cup (175 mL) plain yogurt and serve immediately.
Makes 2 cups (500 mL).

Chapter Eight

Salsa
Sensations

R ARELY do we open a food magazine without finding a mention of salsa. Best described as the name given to a Mexican sauce, salsas are either cooked or fresh mixtures of fruits and vegetables. The more salsas we make, the better we like them. And they have so many uses! Spicy or mild, chunky or smooth, and in colours of gold, green or red, salsas transform an otherwise plain meal into a dinner to remember.

Chile peppers of one type or another are usually added to salsa for flavour and to give authenticity. Some chiles can be positively fiery while others are quite mild. Just how mouth-searing a chile is depends on the amount of capsaicin, an acidic chemical, concentrated in the veins and seeds. That's why removing veins and seeds lowers the heat level. As a rule of thumb, the smaller and more pointed the chile, the hotter it is. And remember, be sure to wear rubber gloves when handling all hot chile peppers

Tomatillos are another Mexican specialty. We love to make our Tomatillo Mexican Salsa (page 129) whenever they are available. Fresh cilantro also gives an authentic Mexican flavour to salsa. It is easily found today in supermarkets, sometimes referred to as Chinese parsley, other times as fresh coriander.

"Fusion" cooking, a crossover of different cuisines, is showing up in salsas as well. Try our Asian Salsa (page 133) for a salsa with a difference.

Fresh vegetable and fresh fruit salsas are interesting variations on the salsa theme. Best made close to serving time, they add a burst of flavour to otherwise ordinary foods.

Serving Suggestions

Salsas really jazz up plain old ground beef, whether in a meat loaf or in patties. Fajitas wouldn't be fajitas without salsa. Add some salsa to low-fat sour cream or plain yogurt to make a light dip. And perhaps the best way to eat salsa is alone with your favourite dippers!

List of Recipes

Southwest Salsa

Here is your basic recipe for salsa. The original asked for the juice of a Seville orange. Since these bitter oranges are not always available, we substituted a blend of lime and sweet orange juice. The salsa is best made when field-ripened tomatoes are in season. Make enough to last till they are again available!

4 cups	chopped peeled tomatoes (about 2 lb/1 kg)	1 L
1 cup	chopped onion	250 mL
3	cloves garlic, minced	3
½ cup	chopped sweet red pepper	125 mL
2–4	jalapeño peppers, seeded and minced (see Tips)	2–4
½ cup	red wine vinegar	125 mL
¼ cup	chopped fresh cilantro (see Tips)	50 mL
2 tbsp	orange juice	25 mL
1 tbsp	lime juice	15 mL
1 tsp	each: granulated sugar and pickling salt	5 mL
¼ cup	tomato paste	50 mL

1. Combine tomatoes, onion, garlic, peppers, vinegar, cilantro, orange and lime juice, sugar and salt in a large stainless steel or enamel saucepan. Bring to a boil over high heat, reduce heat and boil gently, uncovered, for 30 minutes or until mixture is thickened, stirring occasionally. Stir in tomato paste and cook for 2 minutes.
2. Remove hot jars from canner and ladle salsa into jars to within ½ inch (1 cm) of rim (head space). Process for 20 minutes for half-pint (250 mL) jars and for pint (500 mL) jars as directed on page 93 (Longer Time Processing Procedure).

Makes 4 cups (1 L).

Tips:

Jalapeño peppers vary in heat level—you may wish less or more depending on your preference.

Cilantro is perhaps the world's most popular herb. It really makes salsa sing. Store fresh cilantro with its root ends in water and covered with a plastic bag. Change the water every few days. Wash the cilantro and remove the root ends just before using.

Beyond Hot Salsa

Commonly known as *picante*, this salsa is not for the timid. If it's too *picante* for your taste, cut the heat by reducing the amount of jalapeño and red hot chile peppers. If it's not *picante* enough, be our guest and add more.

8	plum tomatoes	8
1	large onion	1
4	large cloves garlic	4
4–5	jalapeño peppers, seeded (see Tip)	4–5
2	small red hot chile peppers, seeded	2
¼ cup	cider vinegar	50 mL
2 tsp	dried oregano leaves or 2 tbsp (25 mL) fresh	10 mL
1 tsp	each: pickling salt and granulated sugar	5 mL

1. Combine tomatoes, onion, garlic and peppers in a food processor or blender; process until smooth. Transfer to a medium stainless steel or enamel saucepan.
2. Add vinegar, oregano, salt and sugar. Bring to a boil over high heat, reduce heat and boil gently, uncovered, for about 15 minutes or until the salsa is thickened.
3. Remove hot jars from canner and ladle salsa into jars to within ½ inch (1 cm) of top rim (head space). Process for 20 minutes for half pint (250 mL) jars and pint (500 mL) jars as directed on page 93 (Longer Time Processing Procedure).

Makes 3 cups (750 mL).

Tip: Jalapeño peppers vary in heat level from hot to very hot, but you cannot tell the heat level from their appearance.

Gazpacho Salsa

Gazpacho, that great Spanish cold soup from Andalucia, always makes us think of summertime. So does this salsa. However, this salsa can be made anytime but the flavours are always at their best in summer, when garden-ripened produce is used.

1 tbsp	olive oil	15 mL
½ cup	finely chopped onion	125 mL
2	cloves garlic, minced	2
4	large tomatoes, peeled and chopped (about 3 cups/750 mL)	4
½ cup	diced peeled seedless cucumber	125 mL
½ cup	diced sweet green pepper	125 mL
2 cups	tomato juice	500 mL
⅓ cup	red wine vinegar	75 mL
1 tbsp	Worcestershire sauce	15 mL
1 tsp	each: ground cumin and paprika	5 mL
2 tbsp	chopped fresh basil	25 mL
	Salt and freshly ground pepper, to taste	

1. Heat oil in a medium stainless steel or enamel saucepan and sauté onion on medium heat for 5 minutes. Add garlic and cook for 1 minute.
2. Stir in tomatoes, cucumber, green pepper, tomato juice, vinegar, Worcestershire sauce, cumin and paprika. Bring to a boil over high heat, reduce heat and boil gently, uncovered, for about 30 minutes or until mixture is thickened, stirring occasionally. Stir in basil, salt and pepper and cook for 2 minutes.
3. Remove hot jars from canner and ladle salsa into jars to within ½ inch (1 cm) of rim (head space). Process for 20 minutes for half-pint (250 mL) jars and pint (500 mL) jars as directed on page 93 (Longer Time Processing Procedure).

Makes 4 cups (1 L).

Tip: Salsas are so popular, you will probably find yourself using them with beef or chicken fajitas and with all types of fish.

Tomatillo Mexican Salsa

Tomatillos are finding favour with salsa lovers for their fresh tart flavour and hint of lemon and apple. These little green fruits are covered with a thin papery husk. They belong to the same family as tomatoes and the cape gooseberry. Popular in Mexican and Southwestern cooking, they make one of our favourite salsas. Choose tomatillos that have their husks intact and are still green. They may be kept in a paper bag in the refrigerator for up to a month. If you can't find tomatillos, green tomatoes may be substituted. Choose pale green rather than dark green tomatoes to avoid solanine, a potentially toxic substance that disappears as the tomato ripens.

½ lb	tomatillos (about 7 tomatillos)	250 g
2	hot green chile peppers, seeded and chopped	2
2	cloves garlic, minced	2
½ cup	chopped sweet red pepper	125 mL
½ cup	chopped onion	125 mL
½ cup	chopped carrot	125 mL
¼ cup	each: apple juice and cider vinegar	50 mL
¾ tsp	pickling salt	4 mL
½ tsp	each: ground cumin and dried oregano	2 mL
1 tbsp	granulated sugar	15 mL

1. Remove husks from tomatillos and discard. Wash tomatillos and coarsely chop in a food processor or by hand. Transfer to a medium stainless steel or enamel saucepan; add chiles, garlic, red pepper, onion, carrot, apple juice, vinegar, salt, cumin and oregano. Bring to a boil over high heat, reduce heat, cover and boil gently for 10 minutes.
2. Stir in sugar, return to a boil and boil gently, uncovered, for 20 minutes or until mixture is thickened. Remove from heat.
3. Remove hot jars from canner and ladle salsa into jars to within ½ inch (1 cm) of rim (head space). Process 20 minutes for half-pint (250 mL) jars and pint (500 mL) jars as directed on page 93 (Longer Time Processing Procedure).

Makes 2 cups (500 mL).

Fresh and Dried Cranberry Salsa

Dried cranberries are added to fresh or frozen ones in this salsa to create a more concentrated cranberry flavour. They are then cooked with the rest of the ingredients to bring out their best flavour. Use this salsa as an alternative to cranberry sauce or jelly.

1 cup	fresh or frozen cranberries, coarsely chopped	250 mL
¼ cup	dried cranberries	50 mL
¼ cup	chopped red onion	50 mL
2 tbsp	chopped fresh parsley	25 mL
1–2 tbsp	liquid honey	15–25 mL
1 tbsp	each: red wine vinegar and lemon juice	15 mL
2 tsp	granulated sugar	10 mL
¼ tsp	each: pickling salt and hot pepper flakes	1 mL

1. Combine cranberries, onion, parsley, honey, vinegar, lemon juice, sugar, salt and pepper flakes in a medium stainless steel or enamel saucepan. Bring to a boil over medium heat, reduce heat and boil gently, uncovered, for about 10 minutes or until mixture is thickened, stirring frequently.
2. Remove hot jars from canner and ladle salsa into jars to within ½ inch (1 cm) of rim (head space). Process for 20 minutes for half-pint (250 mL) jars and for pint (500 mL) jars as directed on page 93 (Longer Time Processing Procedure).

Makes 1¼ cups (300 mL).

Tip: Extra honey may be added if a sweeter salsa is desired.

Cranberry Salad Dressing
Combine ½ cup (125 mL) Fresh and Dried Cranberry Salsa, ¼ cup (50 mL) red wine vinegar, 3 tbsp (45 mL) extra virgin olive oil, 1 clove garlic, minced, pinch of salt and pinch of freshly ground pepper in a tightly sealed container. Shake well to blend. Store in the refrigerator. Makes ¾ cup (175 mL).

Fiery Yellow Pepper Salsa

This salsa has lots of heat. If you don't like your salsa this hot, use more sweet pepper in place of the hot ones. Just don't change the total amount of peppers. Remember that the heat of individual peppers can vary greatly. This salsa is a peppery dip for nacho chips or a bold accompaniment to grilled chicken, beef or pork.

2 cups	chopped sweet yellow pepper	500 mL
2 cups	chopped peeled ripe tomatoes	500 mL
	(about 2 medium tomatoes)	
½ cup	finely chopped red onion	125 mL
¼ cup	finely chopped hot yellow pepper	50 mL
¼ cup	finely chopped jalapeño pepper	50 mL
2	large cloves garlic, minced	2
¼ cup	lime juice	50 mL
2 tbsp	white vinegar	25 mL
½ tsp	pickling salt	2 mL
2 tbsp	finely chopped fresh cilantro	25 mL

1. Combine sweet pepper, tomatoes, onion, hot peppers, garlic, lime juice, vinegar and salt in a medium stainless steel or enamel saucepan. Bring to a boil over high heat, reduce heat and boil gently, uncovered, for about 15 minutes or until mixture is thickened, stirring frequently. Stir in cilantro and cook for 2 minutes.
2. Remove hot jars from canner and ladle sauce into jars to within ½ inch (1 cm) of rim (head space). Process 20 minutes for half-pint (250 mL) jars and pint (500 mL) jars as directed on page 93 (Longer Time Processing Procedure).

Makes 3 cups (750 mL).

Tomato Salsa Tortillas

Add a new twist to Sunday brunch. Serve tortillas! Roll them up with scrambled eggs and top with a Fresh Vegetable Salsa (pages 134–137). It's the perfect way to start a week.
Heat 1 tbsp (15 mL) butter or margarine in a large skillet. Add 2 chopped green onions and 6 sliced mushrooms; sauté for 5 minutes. Beat 5 eggs with 2 tbsp (25 mL) milk and salt and pepper to taste. Pour into skillet and scramble eggs until soft, about 5 minutes. Add 2 chopped tomatoes and cook for 2 minutes. Place one quarter of filling on each of 4 tortillas, roll up and place seam-side down. Spoon your choice of salsa on top. Serve immediately. Makes 4 servings.

Peach Mint Salsa

The sunny taste of peaches and the cool freshness of mint combine in this lovely fruit salsa to say "summer." Make this quick salsa when peaches are at their flavour peak. Its fresh taste beautifully complements grilled chicken and fish.

2 cups	chopped peeled peaches	500 mL
	(about 4 medium peaches)	
¼ cup	finely chopped red onion	50 mL
¼ cup	finely chopped sweet green pepper	50 mL
1 tbsp	finely chopped jalapeño pepper	15 mL
2 tbsp	liquid honey	25 mL
¼ tsp	pickling salt	1 mL
	Grated rind and juice of 1 lime	
2 tbsp	finely chopped fresh mint	25 mL

1. Combine peaches, onion, peppers, honey, salt, lime rind and juice in a small stainless steel or enamel saucepan. Bring to a boil over high heat, reduce heat and boil gently, uncovered, for 5 minutes, stirring occasionally.
2. Stir in mint and cook for 1 minute.
3. Remove hot jars from canner and ladle salsa into jars to within ½ inch (1 cm) of rim (head space). Process for 10 minutes for half-pint (250 mL) or pint (500 mL) jars as directed on page 93 (Longer Time Processing Procedure).

Makes 2 cups (500 mL).

Asian Salsa

Fusion cooking is not new. But when it stretches into Mexican/Asian, look out for a rather special salsa. Serve as you would any other salsa.

½	lemon	½
½	orange	½
1	medium onion	1
1	clove garlic, crushed	1
1	large apple, peeled and cored	1
1	can (28 oz/798 mL) tomatoes	1
½ cup	cider vinegar	125 mL
¼ cup	lightly packed brown sugar	50 mL
1	cinnamon stick, 4 inches (10 cm) long	1
3	cardamom pods	3
1 tbsp	chopped gingerroot	15 mL
1–2 tbsp	soy sauce	15–25 mL
½ tsp	each: salt and ground allspice	2 mL

1. Chop lemon and orange in a food processor with on/off motion until very fine. Remove to a medium stainless steel or enamel saucepan. Chop onion, garlic and apple and add to saucepan. Stir in tomatoes, vinegar, sugar, cinnamon stick, cardamom and gingerroot.
2. Bring mixture to a boil over high heat, reduce heat and boil gently, uncovered, for about 25 minutes or until mixture is thickened. Stir in soy sauce, salt and allspice and remove cinnamon stick.
3. Remove hot jars from canner and ladle sauce into jars to within ½ inch (1 cm) of rim (head space). Process for 20 minutes for half-pint (250 mL) jars and for pint (500 mL) jars as directed on page 93 (Longer Time Processing Procedure).

Makes 4 cups (1 L).

Fresh Salsas

Salsas originated in Mexico, where they are always served fresh and so are best eaten immediately or at the most in a day or two. Fresh tomato salsas are by far the most common, but more and more ingredients, particularly fruits and other vegetables, are finding their way into this popular condiment.

Triple Tomato Salsa

Three kinds of tomatoes—cherry, tomatillo and common—are the basis of this appealing salsa. It has become one of our favourite dips for tortilla chips. If you can find orange or yellow cherry tomatoes, they add interesting colour.

1 tbsp	extra virgin olive oil	15 mL
½ cup	chopped red onion	125 mL
2 tbsp	dry white wine	25 mL
8	green tomatillos, husked, cored and diced (see Tip)	8
4	ripe medium tomatoes, seeded and diced	4
2 cups	yellow, orange or red cherry tomatoes, diced	500 mL
	Salt and freshly ground pepper	
6	sprigs fresh basil, chopped	6

1. Heat oil in a large non-stick skillet over medium-high heat. Add onion and cook for 2 minutes. Add wine and tomatillos; stir to combine. Remove from heat.
2. Add tomatoes to skillet while it is still warm. Season to taste with salt and pepper; stir in basil.
3. Place mixture in a medium bowl. Cover and let stand for 20 minutes. Refrigerate until serving time, but use within 6 hours.

Makes 3 cups (750 mL).

Tip: If you are unable to buy tomatillos, replace with diced pale green tomatoes.

Tomato Basil Salsa

A Foodland Ontario recipe inspired this salsa. We like to make it when great field tomatoes and lots of fresh basil are plentiful. Enjoy it with cooked fettucine, fusilli or shell pasta topped with freshly grated Parmesan cheese.

2 cups	chopped unpeeled tomatoes (about 2 large tomatoes)	500 mL
¾ cup	chopped fresh basil	175 mL
½ cup	finely chopped red onion	125 mL
¼ cup	tomato paste	50 mL
2	cloves garlic, crushed	2
2 tbsp	Dijon mustard	25 mL
2 tbsp	sherry or red wine vinegar	25 mL
1 tbsp	walnut or vegetable oil	15 mL

Combine tomatoes, basil, onion, tomato paste, garlic, mustard, vinegar and oil in a small bowl. Cover and let stand at room temperature for several hours. Or place in plastic containers with tight-fitting lids and freeze for longer storage.

Makes about 2½ cups (625 mL).

Garlic Tomato Salsa

An easy-to-make fresh salsa chock full of flavour. Even non-garlic lovers may become addicted.

2	ripe medium tomatoes, chopped	2
2	cloves garlic, crushed	2
2 tbsp	lime juice	25 mL
1 tbsp	chopped fresh cilantro or parsley	15 mL
1 tbsp	finely chopped red onion	15 mL
1 tsp	capers, drained and chopped	5 mL
⅛ tsp	salt	0.5 mL

Combine tomatoes, garlic, lime juice, cilantro, onion, capers and salt in a small bowl. Cover and let stand in refrigerator for 15 minutes.

Makes 1 cup (250 mL).

Roasted Corn and Sweet Pepper Salsa

Roasting sweet corn caramelizes the sugar in the kernels into a wonderful woodsy flavour that is highlighted by balsamic vinegar and sweet peppers.

1½ cups	fresh corn kernels (about 3 ears)	375 mL
1 tsp	olive oil	5 mL
¼ cup	each: diced sweet orange pepper and sweet green pepper	50 mL
¼ cup	diced red onion	50 mL
2 tbsp	chopped fresh Italian parsley	25 mL
2 tsp	each: balsamic vinegar and lime juice	10 mL
⅛ tsp	salt	0.5 mL

1. Heat a large non-stick skillet over medium-high heat. Add corn and oil and cook until corn turns a light brown, stirring constantly. Remove from heat and cool for 5 minutes.
2. Stir in peppers, onion, parsley, vinegar, lime juice and salt. Cover and let stand for 30 minutes before serving.

Makes 1½ cups (375 mL).

Mango Cilantro Salsa

Make this salsa whenever fresh mangoes are plentiful and inexpensive, usually from mid June till the end of July.

1	ripe medium mango	1
3 tbsp	chopped fresh cilantro	45 mL
2	green onions, thinly sliced	2
1–2 tbsp	finely chopped jalapeño pepper	15–25 mL
1 tsp	lime juice	5 mL
½ tsp	granulated sugar	2 mL
⅛ tsp	each: salt and ground ginger	0.5 mL

Peel and dice mango into small pieces. Combine mango, cilantro, onions, jalapeño pepper, lime juice, sugar, salt and ginger in a small bowl. Adjust seasonings, if desired. Serve immediately or cover and refrigerate for up to 1 day.

Makes about 1¼ cups (300 mL).

Fresh Banana Salsa

This salsa is a change from other traditional fruit ones. It uses bananas, which are always readily available. We especially enjoy it with fish.

2	plum tomatoes	2
1	large firm banana	1
½ cup	finely chopped red onion	125 mL
3 tbsp	lemon juice	45 mL
3 tbsp	chopped fresh cilantro	45 mL
2 tsp	brown or granulated sugar	10 mL
	Salt and freshly ground pepper	

Cut tomatoes and banana into small dice and place in a small bowl. Combine onion, lemon juice, cilantro and sugar with tomato mixture. Cover and let stand for about 1 hour or longer. Add salt and pepper to taste.

Makes 2½ cups (625 mL).

Paradise Papaya Salsa

Colourful as well as flavourful, this salsa goes well with fruit salads, cottage cheese and chicken.

2 cups	diced peeled papaya	500 mL
½ cup	chopped sweet red pepper	125 mL
2	green onions, chopped	2
4 tsp	lime juice	20 mL
2 tsp	balsamic vinegar	10 mL
1	clove garlic, minced	1
	Salt and freshly ground pepper	

Combine papaya, red pepper, onions, lime juice, vinegar and garlic. Cover and let stand for about 1 hour. Add salt and pepper to taste.

Makes 2½ cups (625 mL).

Tri-Colour Citrus Mint Salsa

Multi-hued citrus gives a pleasing appearance as well as a refreshing flavour to this delightful salsa. It is particularly good with fish and chicken entrées.

2	medium pink grapefruit	2
2	large oranges	2
2	limes	2
1	jalapeño pepper, seeded and minced	1
2 tsp	finely minced shallots	10 mL
1 tsp	liquid honey	5 mL
⅛ tsp	salt	0.5 mL
3–4 drops	hot pepper sauce	3–4 drops

1. Remove outside rind from grapefruit, oranges and limes with a sharp knife, exposing the pulp of the fruit. Carefully cut on both sides of each inner membrane and gently lift out fruit sections. Cut each section into several pieces and place in a bowl. Drain off extra juice and reserve for another use.
2. Stir in pepper, shallots, honey, salt and hot pepper sauce. Refrigerate for about an hour to allow flavours to blend. Salsa may be prepared up to 1 day ahead.

Makes 2 cups (500 mL).

Chapter Nine

Choice Chutneys

C HUTNEYS offer a whole new dimension to foods. Whereas salsas have a light and fresh, lively taste, chutneys have a rich, smooth, mellow, sweet-sour taste. They are a perfect accompaniment to spicy and strong-flavoured foods. Like salsas, chutneys can range in texture from chunky to smooth and in spiciness from mild to hot.

Since dried fruits are often a main ingredient, many chutneys can be made at any time of the year. Chopping can be done with a food processor because all the ingredients become very soft during the cooking. Slow, long cooking is the general rule in making chutneys in order to develop their mellow flavour. And chutneys truly do get better with age, so allow a few weeks in the jar after processing.

Mango chutney is probably the best known of all the chutneys. The addition of papaya in our Mango Papaya Chutney (page 145) is a new approach to this all-time favourite. Hellfire Chutney (page 151), a unique chutney made from dried dates, is probably our most authentic recipe since it was brought with a family moving to Canada from India where chutneys were first known. Juniper Berry Chutney (page 148) has Scottish origins.

Serving Suggestions

Serve one of the lighter chutneys like Apple Plum Chutney or Strawberry Orange Chutney (pages 141 and 142) with roast ham. Chutneys are the traditional accompaniment to hot curried dishes. Fruit flavours in the chutney help take the "sting" from hot foods. Sweeter chutneys, like Sun-Dried Tomato Chutney (page 147) make delicious cracker and bread companions and partner well with cheeses. A salad buffet with cold cuts should offer several chutneys.

List of Recipes

Apple Plum Chutney

Autumn flavours of apples, blue plums and tomatoes shine in this traditionally spiced chutney.

5 cups	chopped peeled and cored apples (about 5 medium apples)	1.25 L
2½ cups	chopped peeled tomatoes (about 3 large tomatoes)	625 mL
2 cups	chopped pitted blue plums (about 8–10 plums)	500 mL
2 cups	sultana raisins	500 mL
2 cups	cider vinegar	500 mL
⅔ cup	chopped onion	150 mL
2	cloves garlic, minced	2
2½ cups	demerara or lightly packed dark brown sugar	625 mL
2 tsp	curry powder	10 mL
¼ tsp	ground allspice	1 mL
¼ tsp	pickling salt	1 mL
⅛ tsp	cayenne	0.5 mL

1. Combine apples, tomatoes, plums, raisins, vinegar, onion and garlic in a large stainless steel or enamel saucepan. Bring to a boil over high heat, reduce heat and boil gently, uncovered, for 30 minutes.
2. Add sugar, return to a boil and boil gently for 30 minutes or until thickened, stirring occasionally. Add curry powder, allspice, salt and cayenne; cook for 5 minutes, stirring frequently.
3. Remove hot jars from canner and ladle chutney into jars to within ½ inch (1 cm) of rim (head space). Process for 10 minutes for half-pint (250 mL) jars and 15 minutes for pint (500 mL) jars as directed on page 93 (Longer Time Processing Procedure).

Makes about 6 cups (1.5 L).

Strawberry Orange Chutney

Make this superb chutney whenever you are able to get great strawberries. Golden raisins and strawberry jam make a fast-to-prepare version. Brushed on ham, turkey or roast pork, it seals in juices during baking and adds its own unique taste. You'll also find it quite wonderful served with plain crackers and a Stilton or blue cheese.

¾ cup	chopped orange (1 medium orange)	175 mL
½ cup	golden raisins	125 mL
½ cup	lightly packed brown sugar	125 mL
½ cup	strawberry jam	125 mL
½ cup	orange juice	125 mL
¼ cup	rice vinegar	50 mL
2 tsp	finely chopped gingerroot	10 mL
1 tsp	ground curry powder	5 mL
2 cups	sliced strawberries	500 mL
½ cup	slivered almonds	125 mL

1. Combine orange, raisins, sugar, jam, orange juice, vinegar, gingerroot and curry in a medium stainless steel or enamel saucepan. Bring to a boil over high heat, reduce heat and boil gently, uncovered, for 15 minutes or until slightly thickened, stirring frequently.
2. Add strawberries, return to a boil and boil gently for about 5 minutes or until thickened, stirring occasionally. Remove from heat and stir in almonds.
3. Remove hot jars from canner and ladle chutney into jars to within ½ inch (1 cm) of rim (head space). Process for 20 minutes for half-pint (250 mL) jars as directed on page 93 (Longer Time Processing Procedure).

Makes 2 cups (500 mL).

Cherry Currant Chutney

Rich and thick, this exciting combination of cherries, currants and peppers makes an exquisite accompaniment to duck, roasted turkey and chicken, and even to sausages.

1	medium orange	1
3 cups	fresh or frozen chopped cherries	750 mL
¾ cup	finely chopped onion	175 mL
½	finely chopped sweet green pepper	½
½	finely chopped sweet red pepper	½
⅓ cup	dried currants	75 mL
½ cup	lightly packed brown sugar	125 mL
¼ cup	balsamic vinegar	50 mL
1	1-inch (2.5-cm) piece gingerroot, peeled and chopped	1
¼–½ tsp	dried red pepper flakes	1–2 mL
½ tsp	each: ground cardamom and salt	2 mL
¼ tsp	ground allspice	1 mL

1. Remove 3 thin strips, about 2 inches (5 cm) long, of outer rind from orange and finely chop; reserve orange pulp for another use. Combine rind, cherries, onion, peppers, currants, sugar, vinegar, gingerroot and seasonings in a large stainless steel or enamel saucepan. Bring to a boil, reduce heat and boil gently, covered, for 20 minutes. Uncover and continue to boil gently for 30 minutes or until thickened, stirring frequently.
2. Remove hot jars from canner and ladle chutney into jars to within ½ inch (1 cm) of rim (head space). Process for 10 minutes for half-pint (250 mL) jars and 15 minutes for pint (500 mL) jars as directed on page 93 (Longer Time Processing Procedure).

Makes about 2 cups (500 mL).

Chicken Breast with Cherry Currant Chutney
Coat boneless chicken breasts lightly with chutney mixed with water to thin to spreading consistency. Bake in a 350°F (180°C) oven for about 20 minutes or until chicken is no longer pink and juices run clear. Pork chops may also receive a similar treatment.

Rhubarb, Date and Apricot Chutney

Dates and apricots give a rich flavour to the sweet-sour taste of rhubarb. It pairs especially well with ham, but also complements other dishes.

4 cups	sliced rhubarb	1 L
1 cup	chopped dried dates	250 mL
1 cup	lightly packed brown sugar	250 mL
½ cup	chopped dried apricots	125 mL
½ cup	cider vinegar	125 mL
¼ cup	finely chopped onion	50 mL
¼ cup	finely chopped crystallized ginger (page 196)	50 mL
1 tsp	curry powder	5 mL
¼ tsp	ground nutmeg	1 mL
¼ tsp	pickling salt	1 mL

1. Combine rhubarb, dates, sugar, apricots, vinegar, onion, ginger, curry powder, nutmeg and salt in a large stainless steel or enamel saucepan. Bring to a boil over medium–high heat; reduce heat and cook, uncovered, for 8 minutes, or until thickened and fruit is soft, stirring frequently.
2. Remove hot jars from canner and ladle chutney into jars to within ½ inch (1 cm) of rim (head space). Process 10 minutes for half-pint (250 mL) jars and 15 minutes for pint (500 mL) jars as directed on page 93 (Longer Time Processing Procedure).

Makes about 3 cups (750 mL).

Mango Papaya Chutney

These two magnificent tropical fruits, mango and papaya, make this chutney such a wonderful accompaniment to cottage cheese and fruit salad, or to any Caribbean chicken or pork dish. It is also excellent served with fish.

½ cup	granulated sugar	125 mL
¼ cup	water	50 mL
¼ cup	cider vinegar	50 mL
3 cups	finely chopped papaya and mango	750 mL
1–2 tbsp	minced jalapeño or hot yellow peppers	15–25 mL
1 tbsp	minced gingerroot	15 mL
½ tsp	ground coriander	2 mL
¼ tsp	salt	1 mL

1. Combine sugar and water in a heavy stainless steel or enamel saucepan. Bring to a boil, uncovered, over medium–high heat; reduce heat and boil gently for about 8 minutes or until mixture has become syrupy, without stirring.
2. Remove from heat and carefully add vinegar (mixture may bubble). Add papaya, mango, peppers, gingerroot, coriander and salt. Return to a boil, reduce heat to medium low and boil gently for 10 minutes or until fruit is tender and chutney has thickened, stirring occasionally.
3. Remove hot jars from canner and ladle chutney into jars to within ½ inch (1 cm) of rim (head space). Process for 10 minutes for half-pint (250 mL) jars or 15 minutes for pint (500 mL) jars as directed on page 93 (Longer Time Processing Procedure).

Makes about 2¼ cups (550 mL).

Chutney Salad Dressing
Use 2–3 tbsp (25-45 mL) Mango Papaya Chutney with ⅓ cup (75 mL) low-fat plain yogurt as a dressing for torn romaine leaves.

Cranberry Citrus Chutney

While many chutney recipes call for freshly harvested produce, this chutney is made with ingredients readily available in the dead of winter. It's a spicy chutney combining the fruitiness of oranges with the tart freshness of lemons. You'll find it a superb accompaniment to pork and poultry dishes as well as cheddar or cream cheese and crackers.

½	large unpeeled lemon, finely chopped	½
½	large unpeeled orange, finely chopped	½
½ cup	water	125 mL
1	pkg (340 g) fresh or frozen cranberries (or 3½ cups/875 mL)	1
1	medium apple, peeled, cored and chopped	1
¾ cup	lightly packed brown sugar	175 mL
⅓ cup	candied orange peel	75 mL
⅓ cup	candied mixed fruit	75 mL
⅓ cup	cider vinegar	75 mL
¼ cup	red wine	50 mL
3 tbsp	minced gingerroot	45 mL
1½ tsp	mustard seeds	7 mL
½ tsp	each: salt, ground allspice and ground cinnamon	2 mL
¼ tsp	ground cloves	1 mL

1. Combine lemon, orange and water in a medium stainless steel or enamel saucepan. Bring to a boil, reduce heat to low, cover and boil gently for 15 minutes.
2. Add cranberries, apple, sugar, orange peel, mixed fruit, vinegar, wine, gingerroot and spices. Return to a boil, reduce heat and boil gently, uncovered, for 15 minutes or until thickened, stirring frequently.
3. Remove hot jars from canner and ladle chutney into jars to within ½ inch (1 cm) of rim (head space). Process for 10 minutes for half-pint (250 mL) jars and 15 minutes for pint (500 mL) jars as directed on page 93 (Longer Time Processing Procedure).

Makes 3½ cups (875 mL).

Sun-Dried Tomato Chutney

Two kinds of tomatoes, sun-dried and fresh, are used to create this exciting chutney. It has some spice level for further interest. Perfect with cooked rice, pasta, curries and egg and cheese dishes, it can also be served with grilled meats and chicken.

1	can (28 oz/798 mL) diced tomatoes	1
1 cup	finely chopped onion	250 mL
½ cup	chopped sun-dried tomatoes (not oil-packed)	125 mL
½ cup	dried currants	125 mL
½ cup	lightly packed brown sugar	125 mL
½ cup	water	125 mL
¼ cup	balsamic vinegar	50 mL
1	2 inch (5 cm) piece gingerroot, finely chopped	1
2	cloves garlic, minced	2
2 tsp	curry powder	10 mL
¼ tsp	each: salt and hot pepper flakes	1 mL

1. Combine tomatoes, onion, sun-dried tomatoes and currants in a large stainless steel or enamel saucepan. Stir in sugar, water, vinegar, gingerroot, garlic, curry powder, salt and pepper flakes.
2. Bring to a boil over high heat, stirring occasionally. Reduce heat to low and boil gently, uncovered, for 30 minutes or until chutney is very thick, stirring frequently.
3. Remove hot jars from canner and ladle chutney into jars to within ½ inch (1 cm) of rim (head space). Process for 10 minutes for half-pint (250 mL) jars and 15 minutes for pint (500 mL) jars as directed on page 93 (Longer Time Processing Procedure).

Makes 3½ cups (875 mL).

Juniper Berry Chutney

This unusual chutney was inspired by a gift jar that Margaret's friend Janine brought her from Scotland. The flavour of juniper berries makes it a natural accompaniment to game, curry dishes and ham. Juniper berries are usually sold dry for flavouring meats, sauces and stuffings.

3	large tomatoes, peeled and chopped (about 2½ cups/625 mL)	3
1	large tart green apple, peeled, cored and chopped	1
1	medium onion, chopped	1
½ cup	sultana raisins	125 mL
½ cup	light brown sugar	125 mL
½ cup	each: liquid honey and cider vinegar	125 mL
¼ cup	water	50 mL
1 tbsp	juniper berries, crushed (see Tips)	15 mL
¼ tsp	salt	1 mL
⅛ tsp	hot pepper sauce	0.5 mL

1. Combine tomatoes, apple, onion, raisins, sugar, honey, vinegar, water and juniper berries in a large stainless steel or enamel saucepan. Bring to a boil over high heat, reduce heat and boil gently, uncovered, for 25 minutes or until thickened, stirring occasionally. Add salt and pepper sauce and cook for 2 minutes.
2. Remove hot jars from canner and ladle chutney into jars to within ½ inch (1 cm) of rim (head space). Process for 10 minutes for half-pint (250 mL) jars and 15 minutes for pint (500 mL) jars as directed on page 93 (Longer Time Processing Procedure).

Makes 4 cups (1 L).

Tips:
Look for juniper berries in specialty or bulk stores carrying a selection of spices.

Crushing the berries helps release their flavour.

Orchard Chutney

Roasted garlic gives richness to this flavourful multi-fruit chutney that always adds interest to everyday meals. Served as an appetizer with soft Brie or Camembert cheese on crackers, it is quite magnificent!

2	heads garlic	2
2½ cups	chopped peeled tart apples (about 3 medium apples)	625 mL
2 cups	chopped peeled peaches (about 4 medium peaches)	500 mL
1 cup	chopped onions	250 mL
1 cup	golden raisins	250 mL
½ cup	chopped dried apricots	125 mL
1 cup	lightly packed brown sugar	250 mL
1¼ cups	cider vinegar	300 mL
¼ cup	balsamic vinegar	50 mL
1 tbsp	finely chopped gingerroot	15 mL
½ tsp	each: ground allspice and pickling salt	2 mL
¼ tsp	ground cloves	1 mL

1. Wrap each head of garlic in a double thickness of foil. Bake in a 400°C (200°C) oven for 40 minutes or until garlic is very soft. Cool and remove foil. With scissors, snip the tip from each clove and carefully squeeze out garlic, removing any pieces of the paper husk. Chop garlic paste finely with a knife.
2. Add garlic, apples, peaches, onions, raisins, apricots, sugar, vinegars, gingerroot, allspice, salt and cloves to a large stainless steel or enamel saucepan. Bring to a boil over high heat, reduce heat and boil gently, uncovered, for 30 minutes or until thickened.
3. Remove hot jars from canner and ladle chutney into jars to within ½ inch (1 cm) of rim (head space). Process 10 minutes for half-pint (250 mL) jars and pint (500 mL) jars as directed on page 93 (Longer Time Processing Procedure).

Makes 5½ cups (1.375 L).

Red Pepper Apricot Chutney

This light, fresh chutney goes well with pork curries, and with duck, poultry and lamb. Enjoy it in a cheddar cheese sandwich or with cream cheese and melba toast. Wonderful plump Turkish apricots for this recipe are readily found in most food stores.

1 cup	diced sweet red pepper (about ½ large pepper)	250 mL
1 cup	chopped dried apricots	250 mL
¾ cup	chopped onion	175 mL
1	apple, peeled, cored and chopped (1 cup/250 mL)	1
⅔ cup	granulated sugar	150 mL
½ cup	golden raisins	125 mL
½ cup	cider vinegar	125 mL
¼ cup	water	50 mL
1 tbsp	minced crystallized ginger (page 196)	15 mL
¼ tsp	each: ground cinnamon, mace and salt	1 mL
⅛ tsp	cayenne	0.5 mL

1. Combine red pepper, apricots, onion, apple, sugar, raisins, vinegar, water and ginger in a medium stainless steel or enamel saucepan. Bring to a boil over high heat, reduce heat, cover and boil gently for 10 minutes, stirring occasionally. Add cinnamon, mace, salt and cayenne. Cook, uncovered, for about 5 minutes, stirring frequently.
2. Remove hot jars from canner and ladle chutney into jars to within ½ inch (1 cm) of rim (head space). Process for 10 minutes for half-pint (250 mL) jars and 15 minutes for pint (500 mL) jars as directed on page 93 (Longer Time Processing Procedure).

Makes about 2½ cups (625 mL).

Variation:

Red Pepper Peach Chutney
Replace apricots with 1 cup (250 mL) chopped peeled peaches and omit water.

Hellfire Chutney

Margaret's daughter Martha learned of this unusual chutney from her friend Patricia. Patricia's mother, Yvonne LeFebour, brought the recipe with her when she moved from India to Toronto. She generously shares it with us. You'll find it wonderful served with rice dishes and curries. But don't let the name frighten you. You control the amount of spicing and the resulting hellfire.

1 lb	pitted dates, cut up	500 g
1¾ cups	white vinegar, divided	425 mL
¾ cup	granulated sugar	175 mL
½–1 tsp	cayenne pepper (see Tip)	2–5 mL
¾ tsp	each: ground cinnamon and ground ginger	4 mL
¼ tsp	each: ground cloves and salt	1 mL
3 tbsp	liquid honey	45 mL

1. Place dates in a saucepan with 1½ cups (375 mL) vinegar and allow to soak for 30 minutes. Bring to a boil over medium–high heat, reduce heat to low and cook, covered, for 10 minutes or until dates are tender. Remove from heat and cool. Place in a food processor and purée until smooth.
2. Return mixture to saucepan; add sugar, cayenne, cinnamon, ginger, cloves, salt, honey and remaining ¼ cup (50 mL) vinegar. Cook, uncovered, over low heat until hot, about 5 minutes, stirring constantly.
3. Remove hot jars from canner and ladle chutney into jars to within ½ inch (1 cm) of rim (head space). Process for 10 minutes for half-pint (250 mL) jars and 15 minutes for pint (500 mL) jars as directed on page 93 (Longer Time Processing Procedure).

Makes 3½ cups (875 mL).

Tip: As everyone knows, cayenne pepper is very hot. Add at your own discretion to suit your own taste.

Roasted Tomato Chutney

Roasting the ingredients gives this chutney a nice mellow, roasted taste that is unusual in chutneys. Serve on cooked pasta, with crackers, as an appetizer or in a pasta salad. It also matches well with grilled beef, chicken or pork. Since this chutney is not processed, it must be frozen for longer storage. So make lots and freeze it when plum tomatoes are in season and inexpensive.

1 cup	fresh cilantro leaves, packed tightly	250 mL
10	plum tomatoes, quartered (see Tips)	10
10	cloves garlic, peeled	10
1	2 inch (5 cm) piece hot yellow or jalapeño pepper	1
2 tbsp	olive oil	25 mL
½ tsp	each: ground cumin, mustard seeds, salt and freshly ground pepper	2 mL

1. Place cilantro in a shallow ovenproof casserole. Top with tomatoes, garlic and hot pepper. Drizzle with oil and sprinkle with seasonings.
2. Roast, uncovered, in a 350°F (180°C) oven for about 35 minutes. Remove from oven, stir to combine and cool slightly. Place in a food processor and pulse with on/off motion until coarsely chopped.
3. Spoon chutney into jars or plastic containers to within ½ inch (1 cm) of rim (head space). Cover with tight-fitting lids. Label jars and refrigerate for up to 1 week or freeze for longer storage.

Makes 3 cups (750 mL).

Variation:

Fennel Seed Chutney
Replace mustard seeds with 1 tbsp (15 mL) fennel seeds in Step 1.

Tips:
Tomatoes are best when stored at room temperature. Cold temperatures are usually the "kiss of death" to their fresh flavour and texture. However, if tomatoes are starting to overripen and will be used for cooking, not eating fresh, store them briefly in the refrigerator until you have time to work with them. And, of course, they may be frozen during the bountiful season to use in cooking during the colder months.

   As for green tomatoes, they will ripen if kept out of the refrigerator. So, if you want them to stay green, the refrigerator is the place for them.

Chapter Ten

Savoury Sauces

S AUCES add zest to foods. And the sauces in this chapter are no exception. Tomato sauces, chile sauces, mustards as well as unusual piquant sauces such as Sun-Dried Tomato Tapenade (page 163), each give their own special nuance.

Consider how often in your day-to-day cooking that you open a can of tomato, spaghetti or pizza sauce. Think how nice it would be, instead, to have a variety of these sauces lining your pantry shelves, ready to use in the quantities you require. Our Chunky Basil Pasta Sauce, Roasted Vegetable Pasta Sauce and Seasoned Tomato Sauce (pages 155, 156 and 158) are a start to a useful collection for your pantry shelf.

The pungent flavour of mustard seed has been enhancing food since early Greek and Roman days. The Romans carried mustard north to England, and no English kitchen has since been without it. It was Mr. Coleman, an Englishman, who pounded mustard seed into a fine powder to launch that famous brand. The French combined mustard seed with white wine and spices for the classic Dijon blend, as in Dijon-Style Mustard (page 166).

You can influence the sharpness of the mustard you make by the liquid you use. Mixing mustard with water produces the hottest, sharpest taste by releasing an enzyme in the seed that frees the fiery compounds. Acids such as vinegar or wine give a much milder flavour. Vinegar is used in English-style mustard, Champagne or white wine in Dijon-style mustard, and flat beer is often used by the Chinese. The several kinds of seeds also have different flavours. The darker seeds have a more pungent aroma and flavour.

Serving Suggestions

Brush a sauce such as Summer Sizzle Barbecue Sauce (page 162) or Raspberry Mustard Sauce (page 167) on a simple meat for broiling or outdoor grilling. A serving of plain cooked rice is brightened with a dash of Hoisin-Style Plum Sauce (page 160). Asian Whisky Sauce (page 170) is the best flavour marinade for salmon and swordfish, although we recently tried it on chicken with great results. And of course, no self-respecting meat loaf would be content without some Mango Chile Sauce (page 159).

List of Recipes

Chunky Basil Pasta Sauce

Fall is the time to turn the rich flavours of field-ripened tomatoes and fresh basil into a delicious sauce to have on hand during the winter months. We love it served on fresh pasta and topped with freshly grated Parmesan cheese.

8 cups	coarsely chopped peeled tomatoes (about 9–12 tomatoes or 4 lb/2 kg)	2 L
1 cup	chopped onion	250 mL
3	cloves garlic, minced	3
⅔ cup	red wine	150 mL
⅓ cup	red wine vinegar	75 mL
½ cup	chopped fresh basil	125 mL
1 tbsp	chopped fresh parsley	15 mL
1 tsp	pickling salt	5 mL
½ tsp	granulated sugar	2 mL
1	can (5½ oz/156 mL) tomato paste	1

1. Combine tomatoes, onion, garlic, wine, vinegar, basil, parsley, salt, sugar and tomato paste in a large stainless steel or enamel saucepan. Bring to a boil over high heat, reduce heat to low and simmer, uncovered, for 40 minutes or until mixture reaches desired consistency, stirring frequently.
2. Remove hot jars from canner and ladle sauce into jars to within ½ inch (1 cm) of rim (head space). Process for 35 minutes for pint (500 mL) jars and 40 minutes for quart (1 L) jars as directed on page 93 (Longer Time Processing Procedure).

Makes 8 cups (2 L).

Speedy Pizzas
We also find this sauce useful for making a quick pizza.
Spread Chunky Basil Pasta Sauce over individual or large pizza crusts. Top with your favourite toppings such as pepperoni, chopped green peppers and sliced mushrooms. Sprinkle with shredded mozzarella cheese. Bake in a 350°F (180°C) oven for about 10 minutes or until cheese is bubbly. Cut each pizza into wedges.

Roasted Vegetable Pasta Sauce

Roasting vegetables for this full-flavoured tomato sauce changes a few simple ingredients into an epicurean treat. Serve with linguine or other pasta and a generous sprinkling of freshly grated Parmigiano-Reggiano cheese.

10	plum tomatoes, about 2½ lb (1 kg), unpeeled	10
4	cloves garlic, unpeeled	4
2	small onions, unpeeled	2
1	sweet red pepper	1
¼ cup	balsamic vinegar	50 mL
1 tbsp	chopped fresh oregano or 1 tsp (5 mL) dried	15 mL
1 tsp	granulated sugar	5 mL
1 tsp	salt	5 mL

1. Place tomatoes, garlic, onions and red pepper on a lightly greased baking sheet. Roast in a 450°F (230°C) oven for 45 minutes, removing the garlic after 12 to 15 minutes or when soft. Remove remaining vegetables when they are soft and the skins blistered. Let stand until cool enough to handle.
2. Peel tomatoes, being careful to catch all the juice. Squeeze garlic and onions to remove soft centres. Peel and seed pepper. Place all vegetables in a food processor; process until smooth.
3. Place vegetable purée in a large stainless steel or enamel saucepan. Add vinegar, oregano, sugar and salt. Bring to a boil over high heat, reduce heat, cover and boil for about 15 minutes, stirring frequently.
4. Remove hot jars from canner and ladle sauce into jars to within ½ inch (1 cm) of rim (head space). Process 35 minutes for pint (500 mL) jars and 40 minutes for quart (1 L) jars as directed on page 93 (Longer Time Processing Procedure).

Makes 3½ cups (875 mL).

If cherries are in the freezer or refrigerator, try the Cherry Currant Chutney on page 143.

Blender Ketchup

If you thought ketchup was only for kids, try this adult version and you'll change your mind. Our Blender Ketchup is less sweet and has a fresher tomato flavour than commercial ketchups. It adds zest to casseroles, soups and meat loaves.

7 cups	chopped peeled plum tomatoes, about (4 lb/2 kg)	1.75 L
½ cup	chopped onion	125 mL
½ cup	chopped sweet red pepper	125 mL
⅔ cup	cider vinegar	150 mL
¼ cup	granulated sugar	50 mL
2 tsp	pickling salt	10 mL
1	cinnamon stick, 2 inch (5 cm) long	1
½ tsp	each: whole allspice, whole cloves, peppercorns	2 mL
1	bay leaf	1

1. Combine tomatoes, onion and red pepper in a blender or food processor and process until smooth. Remove to a large stainless steel or enamel saucepan. Bring to a boil over high heat, reduce heat and boil gently, uncovered, for 30 minutes.
2. Add vinegar, sugar and salt. Tie cinnamon, allspice, cloves, peppercorns and bay leaf in cheesecloth and add to saucepan. Return to a boil and boil gently, uncovered, stirring frequently, until volume is reduced by half or until mixture rounds up on a spoon without separation, about 1½ hours. Remove cheesecloth bag.
3. Remove hot jars from canner and ladle ketchup into jars to within ½ inch (1 cm) of rim (head space). Process for 15 minutes for half-pint (250 mL) and pint (500 mL) jars as directed on page 93 (Longer Time Processing Procedure).

Makes about 3 cups (750 mL).

Tip: Dip tomatoes in boiling water for 20–30 seconds so skins will peel easily.

For pickle perfection with asparagus or carrots, see pages 103 and 106.

Seasoned Tomato Sauce

Whenever there is an abundance of tomatoes, it's time to make this fresh-tasting basic sauce. Use it anytime a tomato sauce is called for—in pasta sauces, soups, stews, pizzas or casseroles. Plum tomatoes give the thickest consistency.

12 cups	chopped ripe tomatoes (about 6 lb/3 kg)	3 L
1 cup	chopped onion	250 mL
2	cloves garlic, minced	2
2 tbsp	chopped fresh oregano or	25 mL
	1 tsp (5 mL) dried	
2 tsp	granulated sugar	10 mL
½ tsp	freshly ground black pepper	2 mL
2	bay leaves	2
2 tbsp	lemon juice	25 mL
½ tsp	salt	2 mL

1. Combine tomatoes, onion, garlic, oregano, sugar, pepper and bay leaves in a large stainless steel or enamel saucepan. Bring to a boil over high heat, reduce heat and boil gently, uncovered, until very thick, about 1¼ hours; stir frequently. Press through a food mill or coarse sieve to remove seeds and skins. Add lemon juice and salt.
2. Remove hot jars from canner and ladle sauce into jars to within ½ inch (1 cm) of rim (head space). Process for 35 minutes for half-pint (250 mL) or pint (500 mL) jars as directed on page 93 (Longer Time Processing Procedure).

Makes about 4 cups (1 L).

Quick Sauces
No need to clutter your fridge with an assortment of commercial sauces when this basic sauce is so easily transformed as needed.

Savoury Seafood Sauce: Stir together ½ cup (125 mL) Seasoned Tomato Sauce, 2 tbsp (25 mL) each: lemon juice and prepared horseradish.

Herbed Pizza Sauce: Combine 1 cup (250 mL) Seasoned Tomato Sauce, ½ tsp (2 L) each: dried oregano, dried basil and dried parsley and 1 clove crushed garlic.

Mango Chile Sauce

Mangoes, pineapple juice, rice vinegar and gingerroot blend with traditional ingredients in this flavourful variation. Use it as you would use the traditional sauce. It does wonders to dress up a plain meat loaf.

3 cups	coarsely chopped peeled plum tomatoes (about 6–8 tomatoes or 1½ lb/750 g)	750 mL
2 cups	chopped mango (about 3 mangoes)	500 mL
1	small hot red chile, seeded and finely chopped	1
¾ cup	rice vinegar	175 mL
½ cup	pineapple juice	125 mL
½ cup	each: chopped onion and celery	125 mL
1 tbsp	minced gingerroot	15 mL
3	whole cloves	3
1	bay leaf	1
⅓ cup	granulated sugar	75 mL
½ tsp	pickling salt	2 mL

1. Combine tomatoes, mango, chile, vinegar, pineapple juice, onion, celery, gingerroot, cloves and bay leaf in a large stainless steel or enamel saucepan. Bring to a boil over high heat, reduce heat and boil gently, uncovered, for 1 hour or until thickened, stirring occasionally.
2. Add sugar and salt; return to a boil and boil gently for 10 minutes. Remove and discard bay leaf.
3. Remove hot jars from canner and ladle sauce into jars to within ½ inch (1 cm) of rim (head space). Process 15 minutes for half-pint (250 mL) jars and pint (500 mL) jars as directed on page 93 (Longer Time Processing Procedure).

Makes 4½ cups (1.125 L).

Tip: A mango is ripe when it's fragrant and plump around the stem area, and gives slightly

Hoisin-Style Plum Sauce

Ellie's friend in Australia, Lesley Cook, makes this great sauce as a replacement for bottled hoisin. In addition to being an accompaniment to Asian food, it's delicious as a baste for meat or poultry on the grill. When in a hurry, brush it on chicken pieces and then quickly cook in a microwave oven.

2½ cups	chopped pitted purple plums (about 8–10 plums)	625 mL
1 tbsp	finely chopped gingerroot	15 mL
1	small jalapeño pepper, seeded and cut up	1
2–3	large cloves garlic	2–3
1 cup	cider vinegar	250 mL
½ cup	lightly packed brown sugar	125 mL
¾ tsp	pickling salt	4 mL
¼ tsp	each: ground cloves and ground ginger	1 mL
¼ tsp	freshly ground black pepper	1 mL
⅛ tsp	ground allspice	0.5 mL

1. Place plums, gingerroot, jalapeño pepper, garlic and vinegar in a small stainless steel or enamel saucepan. Bring to a full boil over high heat, reduce heat, cover and boil gently for 15 minutes or until plums are tender. Transfer to a blender or food processor and process until very smooth.
2. Return plum mixture to saucepan and add sugar, salt and spices. Return to a full boil, reduce heat and boil gently, uncovered, for about 40 minutes or until very thick. Stir frequently to prevent sticking.
3. Remove hot jars from canner and ladle sauce into jars to within ½ inch (1 cm) of rim (head space). Process for 10 minutes for half-pint (250 mL) or pint (500 mL) jars as directed on page 93 (Longer Time Processing Procedure).

Makes 2 cups (500 mL).

Maritime Cranberry Sauce

Cranberries, maple and molasses with a dash of rum reflect the maritime traditions of this sauce.

1 cup	orange juice	250 mL
¼ cup	pure maple syrup	50 mL
¼ cup	light molasses	50 mL
2 tbsp	brown sugar	25 mL
¼ tsp	salt	1 mL
3 cups	fresh or frozen cranberries (350 g pkg)	750 mL
1 tbsp	dark rum	15 mL

1. Bring orange juice, maple syrup, molasses, sugar and salt to a boil over medium heat in a medium stainless steel or enamel saucepan. Heat until sugar dissolves.
2. Stir in cranberries, reduce heat and boil gently, uncovered, for 10 minutes or until cranberries pop. Increase heat to medium high and boil for 10 minutes or until mixture is thickened, stirring occasionally. Remove from heat and stir in rum.
3. Remove hot jars from canner and ladle sauce into jars to within ½ inch (1 cm) of rim (head space). Process for 10 minutes for half-pint (250 mL) jars and 15 minutes for pint (500 mL) jars as directed on page 93 (Longer Time Processing Procedure).

Makes about 2 cups (500 mL).

Summer Sizzle Barbecue Sauce

Whether served with beef, chicken and pork, or humble burgers and hot dogs, this barbecue sauce gives meat a real sizzle. When grilling season arrives, in households where it's year round, this is a very valuable sauce to have on hand.

2 tbsp	canola oil	25 mL
2	medium onions, chopped	2
2	large cloves garlic, minced	2
4	large tomatoes, peeled and finely chopped	4
½ cup	dry red wine or beef broth	125 mL
3 tbsp	liquid honey	45 mL
1 tbsp	each: Worcestershire sauce and cider vinegar	15 mL
1 tsp	each: dry mustard and green peppercorns	5 mL
½ tsp	each: chile powder and salt	2 mL
½ cup	tomato sauce	125 mL
1 tbsp	brown sugar	15 mL
¼ tsp	hot pepper sauce	1 mL

1. Heat oil in a large stainless steel or enamel saucepan over medium-high heat. Add onions and garlic and sauté for 5 minutes or until tender, stirring frequently.
2. Add tomatoes, wine, honey, Worcestershire sauce, vinegar, mustard, peppercorns, chile powder and salt. Bring to a boil, reduce heat and boil gently, uncovered, for 30 minutes or until thickened. Remove from heat and purée in a food processor or blender until smooth. Stir in tomato sauce, sugar and pepper sauce, return to saucepan and bring to a boil.
3. Remove hot jars from canner and ladle sauce into jars to within ½ inch (1 cm) of rim. Process for 15 minutes for half-pint (250 mL) jars and for pint (500 mL) jars as directed on page 93 (Longer Time Processing Procedure).

Makes 3 cups (750 mL).

Tip: For an extra heat "hit," add more pepper sauce or cayenne pepper to taste.

Sun-Dried Tomato Tapenade

Replacing traditional olives with sun-dried tomatoes makes this a very different tapenade. Used as a pasta sauce, or on cream or chèvre cheese spread on crackers or crusty French bread, it is superlative.

2 cups	boiling water	500 mL
1 cup	sun-dried tomatoes (not oil-packed), chopped	250 mL
4	cloves garlic	4
⅓ cup	packed fresh basil leaves	75 mL
1 tbsp	olive oil	15 mL
1 tsp	coarse salt	5 mL

1. Pour boiling water over tomatoes in a small bowl; allow to stand for 30 minutes to soften. Drain, reserving ⅓ cup (75 mL) liquid.
2. Place tomatoes, garlic and reserved liquid in a food processor; chop with on/off motion until coarsely chopped. Add basil, oil and salt. Continue to chop until paste-like consistency.
3. Spoon into a tightly sealed container and refrigerate for up to 3 days or freeze for longer storage.

Makes 1 cup (250 mL).

Tomato Tapenade Salad Dressing
Use this sparkling dressing with cabbage slaw, as a topping for sliced tomatoes with a fresh basil garnish, or make it into a dip by adding extra yogurt for raw veggies.
Combine 2 tbsp (25 mL) Sun-Dried Tomato Tapenade with ½ cup (125 mL) light mayonnaise or low-fat plain yogurt.

Melted Brie with Sun-Dried Tomato Tapenade
Remove the rind from a small, round Brie cheese, then spread with 2 tbsp (25 mL) Sun-Dried Tomato Tapenade. Place on a cookie sheet and bake in a 325°F (160°C) oven for about 8 minutes or until cheese just begins to melt.

Puttanesca Freezer Pasta Sauce

This spicy classic Italian sauce is spicy in more ways than one. First, it is well spiced. Second, the name of the sauce is derived from puttana, the Italian word for prostitute. According to one story, the intense aroma and robust flavour of the sauce were like a siren's call to the men who visited these "ladies of pleasure." Another has it that this quick and easy sauce allowed the girls to get on with their work without delay. Whatever the origin, the sauce is delicious served over fresh pasta. Keep some in your freezer for a fast dinner.

¼ cup	extra virgin olive oil	50 mL
1 cup	finely chopped onion	250 mL
4	cloves garlic, minced	4
1	pkg (50 g) anchovy fillets	1
24	plum tomatoes, peeled and chopped	24
1 cup	chopped black olives	250 mL
¼ cup	drained capers, rinsed	50 mL
½ tsp	each: dried oregano and salt	2 mL
¼ tsp	freshly ground black pepper	1 mL

1. Heat oil over medium heat in a large saucepan. Add onion and garlic and cook until soft, about 5 minutes.
2. Drain oil from anchovies into saucepan; finely chop anchovies. Add anchovies, tomatoes, olives, capers, oregano, salt and pepper. Bring to a boil over high heat, reduce heat and cook gently, uncovered, for ¾ hour or until thickened, stirring frequently.
3. Cool sauce, then spoon into freezer containers, cover tightly, label and store in the freezer. Sauce will keep for up to 4 days in the refrigerator.

Makes 6 cups (1.5 L).

Tip: Use two cans (28 oz/798 mL) plum tomatoes when fresh ones are unavailable.

Spinach Pesto Sauce

This recipe extends fresh basil with spinach. Whether you do it to economize, or because basil is in short supply, or because you enjoy its marvellous flavour and fresh bright green colour, it's your choice.

3 cups	torn spinach leaves	750 mL
½ cup	coarsely chopped fresh basil	125 mL
2	cloves garlic, minced	2
3 tbsp	extra virgin olive oil	45 mL
⅓ cup	pine nuts	75 mL
⅓ cup	freshly grated Parmesan cheese	75 mL

1. Process spinach, basil and garlic in a food processor with on/off motion until finely chopped. Slowly add oil and pine nuts; process until blended. Stir in cheese.
2. Transfer to 3 small containers, cover tightly and refrigerate for up to 1 week or freeze for longer storage. One container will serve 2 or 3 people as a pasta sauce.

Makes about 1¼ cups (300 mL) concentrated pesto.

Variations:

Broccoli Pesto Sauce
Adapted from one of Foodland Ontario's recipes, this pesto extends basil with broccoli. Replace spinach with 3 cups (750 mL) cut-up broccoli stems and florets and proceed as above.

Cilantro Pesto Sauce
Replace basil with fresh cilantro.

Tip: The uses for pesto are many. As well as mixing some with hot pasta, try adding a spoonful to oil and vinegar for a vinaigrette, to mayonnaise for a potato or cabbage salad, or to your favourite casserole or stew. We also like it spread on pizza crusts for a quick appetizer or tucked under the skin of chicken before it is grilled. And sliced tomatoes benefit from a small spoonful. For an easy appetizer, see Pesto Appetizer Torta (page 215).

Mustards

Dijon-Style Mustard

This smooth, flavourful mustard compares well to fine commercial Dijon mustards. And it's easy and quick to make. Increase the amount of hot pepper sauce if you want your mustard to have more bite. Mix it with your favourite jam for a sweet and tangy sauce that is perfect for dipping or spreading on meat before broiling. Use it to make the specialty sauces described below. With little effort you can have a refrigerator full of fancy mustards.

¾ cup	dry white wine	175 mL
¼ cup	chopped onion	50 mL
1	small clove garlic, minced	1
½ cup	dry mustard	125 mL
1 tbsp	each: liquid honey and canola oil	15 mL
½ tsp	salt	2 mL
2–3 drops	hot pepper sauce	2–3 drops

1. Combine wine, onion and garlic in a small saucepan. Bring to a boil over high heat, reduce heat and boil gently, uncovered, for 5 minutes. Strain and discard solids.
2. Whisk wine into mustard in a small bowl until well blended. Return to saucepan; add honey, oil, salt and pepper sauce. Bring to a boil and boil gently for 10 minutes to blend flavours and thicken slightly, stirring frequently. Store in a tightly sealed container in the refrigerator for up to 1 month.

Makes ⅔ cup (150 mL).

Honey Lemon Mustard Sauce

Turn Dijon-Style Mustard into a chic sauce to drizzle over steamed vegetables or fish.
Melt ¼ cup (50 mL) butter or margarine in a small saucepan. Stir in 2 tbsp (25 mL) liquid honey, 2 tbsp (25 mL) Dijon-Style Mustard, 1 tbsp (15 mL) lemon juice and 1 tsp (5 mL) grated lemon rind. Cook over low heat until thoroughly heated. Makes about ½ cup (125 mL).

Raspberry Mustard Sauce

Use Dijon-Style Mustard to make this wonderful sauce full of the essence of raspberries. Serve it with ham, make Raspberry Mustard Coating for Chicken (page 222) and, of course, use it to complement the taste of roast pork.

Combine ½ cup (125 mL) Dijon-Style Mustard, 1 tbsp (15 mL) Red Wine Raspberry Vinegar (page 181), ¼ cup (50 mL) crushed raspberries and 2 tsp (10 mL) granulated sugar. Stir well to combine. Store in a tightly sealed container in the refrigerator for up to 1 week. Makes ¾ cup (175 mL).

Savoury Mustard Sauce

Parsley and oregano transform Dijon-Style Mustard into a superb sauce to spread on any kind of meat or cheese sandwich.

Combine ¼ cup (50 mL) Dijon-Style Mustard, 2 tsp (10 mL) chopped fresh parsley, 1 tsp (5 mL) chopped fresh oregano, ½ tsp (2 mL) each: lemon juice and grated lemon rind. Store in a tightly sealed container in the refrigerator for up to two weeks. Makes ¼ cup (50 mL).

Mustard Fruit Dip

Wonderful as a dip for cooked shrimp or chicken cubes.

Combine 2 tbsp (25 mL) Dijon-Style Mustard, ¼ cup (50 mL) chutney (see Chapter 9, pages 141–152) and 2 tsp (10 mL) lemon juice. Makes ⅓ cup (75 mL).

Sun-Dried Tomato Mustard

The subtle sun-dried tomato flavour and interesting coarse texture of this mustard gives a meal extra "zip."

¼ cup	mustard seeds	50 mL
½ cup	chopped sun-dried tomatoes (not oil-packed)	125 mL
¼ cup	balsamic vinegar	50 mL
2 tbsp	dry mustard	25 mL
2 tbsp	extra virgin olive oil	25 mL
1 tsp	salt	5 mL
½ tsp	granulated sugar	2 mL

1. Cover mustard seeds with warm water and refrigerate overnight. Drain and rinse seeds.
2. Place mustard seeds, tomatoes, vinegar, dry mustard, oil, salt and sugar in a food processor. Process until almost smooth and thickened. Store in a tightly sealed container in the refrigerator for up to 1 month or freeze for longer storage.

Makes about 1 cup (250 mL).

Old-Style Whole Seed Mustard

Yellow or brown mustard seeds may be used in this grainy home-style mustard. We like a mixture of both. The brown seeds have a more pungent aroma and flavour than their yellow cousins.

¼ cup	yellow mustard seeds	50 mL
¼ cup	brown mustard seeds	50 mL
½ cup	white wine vinegar	125 mL
1	bay leaf	1
1 tbsp	each: liquid honey and canola oil	15 mL
¼ tsp	salt	1 mL

1. Combine mustard seeds, vinegar and bay leaf and refrigerate for 24 hours. Remove bay leaf and discard.
2. Place seeds and their liquid, honey, oil and salt in a food processor. Process until seeds are broken and mustard is pasty.
3. Store in a tightly sealed container in the refrigerator for up to 1 month or freeze for longer storage.

Makes about 1 cup (250 mL).

Tip: The liquid used to soak the seeds is important to the taste of the mustard. Vinegar gives a mustard with a mild flavour. For a sharper taste, use water to replace the vinegar. This is because water releases an enzyme that reacts with compounds in the seeds to produce the sharp mustard oils. You can also replace vinegar with your favourite wine for a spicier taste or with beer for an extremely hot bite.

Asian Whisky Sauce

Margaret has been using this seafood sauce and marinade since time immemorial, or so it seems. And it never fails to please everyone who tastes it. She uses it for marinating fish fillets as well as whole fish, chicken and pork.

¼ cup	each: canola oil and soy sauce	50 mL
2	cloves garlic, minced	2
½ cup	rye whisky	125 mL
4 tsp	brown sugar	20 mL
¼ tsp	freshly ground pepper	1 mL
	Small piece gingerroot, chopped, optional	

1. Combine oil, soy sauce, garlic, rye whisky, sugar, pepper and gingerroot (if using) in a tightly sealed container. Shake to blend well. Refrigerate until ready to use.

Makes 1 cup (250 mL).

Tip: Use about ⅓ cup (75 mL) of Asian Whisky Sauce to marinate 4 chicken breasts or drumsticks or about 1 lb (500 g) fish or pork. Any unused sauce may be stored in the refrigerator for up to 1 month.

Asian Salmon
Place 4 salmon steaks or 2 fillets in a resealable plastic bag. Pour ½ cup (125 mL) Asian Whisky Sauce over salmon, seal the bag and turn to coat the food evenly. Refrigerate for 1 to 2 hours, turning bag occasionally. Remove salmon from the marinade and grill or broil. Bring the remaining marinade to a boil for 5 minutes, then use to brush on salmon during the cooking. Makes 4 servings.

Asian Cabbage Slaw
Toss shredded cabbage, red or green or both, and chopped green onions with Asian Whisky Sauce. Sprinkle with toasted sesame seeds and refrigerate until ready to serve.

Zippy Horseradish Sauce

Horseradish is so traditional, we decided it was worthwhile making a horseradish sauce to put "under a lid." It turned out to be wonderful, adding a whole new dimension to this humble condiment. The starting strength of your horseradish will determine the "heat" of the finished sauce. It is delicious served with meats and cheeses and especially great on sandwiches. Or fold it into mayonnaise for a peppy dressing for potato or cabbage salad.

1⅓ cups	granulated sugar	325 mL
¾ cup	drained prepared horseradish	175 mL
¾ cup	white wine vinegar	175 mL
¾ cup	water	175 mL
½ tsp	each: salt and paprika	2 mL
¼ cup	chopped fresh parsley	50 mL
¼ tsp	freshly ground pepper	1 mL

1. Combine sugar, horseradish, vinegar, water, salt and paprika in a medium stainless steel or enamel saucepan.
2. Bring to a boil over high heat, reduce heat and boil gently, uncovered, for 10 minutes or until sauce is reduced and no longer runny. Remove from heat, stir in parsley and pepper. Refrigerate in a tightly sealed container for several weeks or freeze for longer storage.

Makes about 1⅓ cups (325 mL).

All Those Extras

Introduction to

All Those Extras

T HIS SECTION contains four chapters, all with recipes that add "extra" interest to the art of canning and preserving food.

Chapter 11, Flavoured Oils and Specialty Vinegars, reflects the current interest in these condiments. Little effort is needed to make these otherwise expensive items in your own kitchen. Using only small amounts in cooking or in marinades gives marvellous results. But safe preparation is of utmost importance in making flavoured oils, particularly as we continue to see publication of unsafe directions. Although the topic was covered well in *Put a Lid on It!*, we think this information is so important it needs repeating. So carefully follow our directions for making flavoured oils (page 174) to enjoy their wonderful flavours without concern about their safety. Unlike the oils, there is no safety issue with the vinegars.

The Finishing Touch, Chapter 12, provides wonderful dessert ideas ranging from fresh fruit salsas to decadent and positively yummy sauces. Most can be processed for future use, while a few are for immediate enjoyment.

In *Put a Lid on It!* we planned to include a chapter for and about kids, but space constraints won out. This time we found room in Chapter 13.

Chapter 14, Let's Open the Lid and Use What's Inside, tells us of many things we can do with the preserves made from the recipes found in the rest of this book. Our suggestions include appetizers and spreads, some breakfast ideas, and a number of baked cakes and squares.

Chapter Eleven

Flavoured Oils and Specialty Vinegars

Flavoured oils and specialty vinegars are currently riding a wave of popularity as a way to enhance the taste of many foods. And because they are so highly flavoured, just a little goes a long way. We love to have them on hand for making a simple vinaigrette, for livening up a marinade or for drizzling over steamed vegetables. The availability of these oils and vinegars in specialty shops is growing, but why pay those high prices when the products are so easily made at home?

Flavoured Oils
Flavoured oils are made by infusing the essence of such foods as garlic, herbs or chile peppers into an oil. We are excited about our new creation in this book, Nut-Infused Oils. You can make a variety of exotic nut oils at a fraction of the expense of the commercial ones.

It is most important when making any flavoured oil to use the proper technique. The problem arises from the ability of *Clostridium botulinum* spores to grow in an oil when a fresh food is present. When conditions are right, the spores can produce a toxin that causes botulism, a virulent form of food poisoning.

Confirmed by Health Canada, our method for making flavoured oils first appeared in *Put a Lid on It!* Any oil with a flavouring essence, such as herbs, garlic or fresh peppers, is heated at a low oven temperature (300°F/150°C) for a specified time. Heating infuses the flavour into the oil and drives out any water in the fresh food. After heating, the oil is cooled slightly and strained, and must be refrigerated thereafter. Be sure to read the Food Safety Alert on page 177.

Flavoured oils add wonderfully interesting flavours to otherwise bland foods and are very easy to make. Follow our instructions closely and you need have no concern about the safety of the resulting oils.

Specialty Vinegars
To make specialty vinegars, we steep fresh herbs and other flavourful produce in a variety of vinegars. Experiment with cider, wine or rice vinegars for the interesting flavours they offer. Poured into a decorative bottle, they make a most attractive gift. Champagne Vinegar (page 180) is one of our favourites and is superb for any elegant occasion. Or, if you really like it, have it every day! Unlike the oils, there is no safety concern with flavoured vinegars, because the high acid nature of vinegar prevents the growth of the botulism organism.

Serving Suggestions

To start a meal with pizzazz, garnish a small dish of a flavoured oil with fresh herbs and serve with pieces of crusty bread for dipping. And be sure to try the Five-Pepper Oil (page 178) on your next pizza. Specialty vinegars dress up tossed greens, pasta and rice salads. We hope you will enjoy one of our homemade vinaigrettes (pages 183–184), using our oils and vinegars. Add one of our flavoured vinegars to a marinade for less tender meat to get flavour as well as tenderness.

List of Recipes

Flavoured Oils

Flavoured oils pack a lot of flavour into just a few drops. They are an excellent way to lower the amount of fat in your diet. Little effort is needed to make these versatile condiments. Be sure to follow the instructions carefully, for if these oils are not made and stored properly, there can be a risk of botulism. Take time to read the introduction on page 174, and then enjoy the wonderful flavours these oils offer with no concern about their safety.

When making the oils, we use either a 2-cup (500-mL) glass measuring cup or a 28-oz (796-mL) can, the size commonly used for canned tomatoes. Many people have glass measuring cups, and the cans are readily available and can be discarded after use, so take your pick. If using the can, remove the top from the can and, after using the contents for another purpose, wash it out and remove the paper label. Cans with labels printed directly on the can are not suitable. Follow the recipe instructions carefully and be sure not to increase the amount of foods you add to the oil, because the heating time is based on the amounts in the recipe. Check that the finished oil is clear and the vegetables blackened. After the oil is strained, if it is cloudy or if there is a separate layer at the bottom of the bottle, the oil was not heated long enough and must be heated until it becomes clear, or it can be refrigerated and used within a week.

Canola, a neutral-tasting oil, is perfect for letting the flavour of added foods come through. However, you may prefer to make the oils using extra virgin olive for the unique taste it provides. Olive oil becomes cloudy with refrigerator storage, but when the oil is slightly warmed, this cloudiness disappears. Just remember with any flavoured oil not to leave it at room temperature for longer than 1 hour and to discard any oil that has sat out for a longer time.

Basil Oil with Lemon and Black Peppercorns

Oil infused with fresh basil has extraordinary flavour, yet is so simple to make. Serve it in a small bowl with a sprinkling of chopped fresh basil and small pieces of crusty French bread for dipping.

1 cup	canola or extra virgin olive oil	250 mL
6	leaves fresh basil	6
2	strips lemon rind, about ½ x 3 inches (1 x 7.5 cm)	2
8	black peppercorns	8

1. Place oil, basil, lemon rind and peppercorns in a 2-cup (500-mL) glass measuring cup or a 28-oz (796-mL) can that has been washed and dried and had the label removed. Set container on a pie plate. Bake in a 300°F (150°C) oven for 90 minutes or until the basil is blackened and crisp. Remove to a rack to cool for 30 minutes.
2. Line a small strainer with a coffee filter or several layers of cheesecloth. Strain oil into a clean glass jar, cover and store in the refrigerator at all times. Use within a month.

Makes about 1 cup (250 mL).

Food Safety Alert: Accurate measurement of the amounts called for in the recipe is essential to making an oil that will not support growth of harmful microorganisms. If you want a larger quantity of oil than one recipe produces, put a second batch of ingredients (a second recipe) into a separate container. Two containers can be heated at the same time in the oven; just don't put more than 1 cup (250 mL) of oil into one or use a smaller container. When the oil has cooled, it is of the utmost importance to keep the oil refrigerated at all times when it's not in use, and to keep it no longer than 1 month. It is a good idea to check the temperature of your oven with an oven thermometer for accuracy.

Oil de Provençe

The flavours of Provençe inspired this excellent and versatile oil. Team it with a mild flavoured vinegar when making a salad vinaigrette.

1 cup	canola or extra virgin olive oil	250 mL
2	strips fresh orange rind (about ½ x 3 inches/1 x 7.5 cm)	2
2	thinly sliced shallots	2
1	bay leaf	1
1 tbsp	chopped fresh thyme leaves or 1 tsp (5 mL) dried	15 mL
1 tsp	fennel seeds	5 mL

1. Place oil, orange rind, shallots, bay leaf, thyme and fennel seeds in a 2-cup (500-mL) glass measuring cup or a 28-oz (796-mL) can that has been washed and dried and had the label removed. Set container on a pie plate. Bake in a 300°F (150°C) oven for 90 minutes or until the shallots are blackened and crisp. Remove to a rack to cool for 30 minutes.
2. Line a small strainer with a coffee filter or several layers of cheesecloth. Strain oil into a clean glass jar, cover and store in the refrigerator at all times. Use within a month.

Makes about 1 cup (250 mL).

Five-Pepper Oil

Five peppers team to give amazing flavour to this powerful oil. Be sure to notice that the increased amount of peppers significantly increases the cooking time. The peppers should be blackened and crisp when the oil is finished.

1	small hot red chile pepper	1
1	habañero chile pepper	1
1	small jalapeño pepper	1
¼	sweet red or orange pepper	¼
8	whole black peppercorns	8
1 cup	canola or extra virgin olive oil	250 mL

1. Remove stems from peppers and cut each in half. Place peppers in a 2-cup (500-mL) glass measuring cup or a 28-oz (796-mL) can that has been washed and dried and had the label removed. Set container on a pie plate. Bake in a 300°F (150°C) oven for 4 hours or until the peppers are blackened and crisp. Remove to a rack to cool for 30 minutes.
2. Line a small strainer with a coffee filter or several layers of cheesecloth. Strain oil into a clean glass jar, cover and store in the refrigerator at all times. Use within a month.

Makes about 1 cup (250 mL).

Dried Porcini Mushroom and Rosemary Oil

In Northern Italy, cooks use ingredients that are readily available. So porcini mushrooms and rosemary, which are kitchen basics, and the ever-available olive oil fit this description. A great oil to brush on pizza shells before adding the toppings.

1 cup	extra virgin olive oil	250 mL
¼ cup	dried porcini mushrooms	50 mL
2	sprigs fresh rosemary or 2 tsp (10 mL) dried	2

1. Place oil, mushrooms and rosemary in a 2-cup (500-mL) glass measuring cup or a 28-oz (796-mL) can that has been washed and dried and had the label removed. Set container on a pie plate. Bake in a 300°F (150°C) oven for 1 hour or until the mushrooms are golden brown. Remove to a rack to cool for 30 minutes.
2. Line a small strainer with a coffee filter or several layers of cheesecloth. Strain oil into a clean jar, cover and store in the refrigerator at all times. Use within a month.

Makes about 1 cup (250 mL).

Nut-Infused Oils

Authentic nut oils are very expensive, but their ambrosial flavour can be reproduced by the following method. We recommend leaving the nuts in the oil after heating to develop a more intense nut flavour. Although oils made with other flavouring essences must always be strained before storing, nut-infused oils can be stored with the nuts and strained just before use, if desired. We love them in a salad dressing with the nuts providing a nice garnish, either in the mixture or sprinkled on top. No doubt you will find other uses for these exotic oils in your own recipes.

| 1 cup | canola oil | 250 mL |
| ¼ cup | chopped nuts, such as walnuts, pecans or hazelnuts or sliced almonds | 50 mL |

1. Place oil and nuts in a 2-cup (500-mL) glass measuring cup or a 28-oz (796-mL) can that has been washed and dried and had the label removed. Set container on a pie plate. Bake in a 300°F (150°C) oven for 1 hour or until the nuts are dark brown. Remove to a rack to cool for 30 minutes.
2. Pour oil and nuts into a clean glass jar, cover and store in the refrigerator at all times. Use within a month.

Makes about 1 cup (250 mL).

Specialty Vinegars

Specialty vinegars enliven a dressing for a tossed green salad and transform a meat or poultry marinade into something memorable. It is most important to start with a good-quality vinegar especially when using wine vinegars. If herbs are used, bruise or crush them to increase their surface area for maximum flavour extraction during steeping. Since flavour declines during storage, it is best to use these specialty vinegars within 6 months after they are made. See page 221 for ideas for marvellous sauces for meats.

Champagne Vinegar

It is truly exciting to be able to use Champagne, the most celebrated of sparkling wines to make a homemade vinegar. So why not celebrate with Champagne Vinegar in a vinaigrette on a salad or splashed over cooked vegetables.

1 cup	dry Champagne	250 mL
1 cup	white wine vinegar	250 mL
1 tsp	granulated sugar	5 mL

1. Bring Champagne, vinegar and sugar just to a boil. Remove from heat and cool slightly. Pour into a clean jar with a tight-fitting lid. Steep in a cool, dark place for several weeks. Store in the refrigerator.

Makes 2 cups (500 mL).

Provençe-Style Vinegar

This recipe first appeared in *Put a Lid on It!* and was one of our most popular vinegars. Its delicate flavour is a perfect partner for salads made from young greens. To retain the flavour after bottling, add 2 fresh strips of orange rind, 1 thyme sprig, a slice shallot, 1 bay leaf and a few fennel seeds.

2 cups	white wine vinegar	500 mL
½ cup	fresh thyme leaves	125 mL
5	wide orange rind strips	5
⅓ cup	thinly sliced dried shallots	75 mL
2	bay leaves	2
2 tsp	fennel seeds	10 mL

1. Bring vinegar to a boil. Wash and dry thyme, then crush or bruise. Place thyme, orange strips, shallots, bay leaves and fennel seeds in a clean jar. Pour vinegar into jar, cover and set in a cool, dark place for several weeks.
2. Taste vinegar and when strength is satisfactory, strain it and discard solids. Pour into a clean jar with a tight-fitting lid. Store in the refrigerator.

Makes 2 cups (500 mL).

Red Wine Raspberry Vinegar

The technique used for this recipe produces a more intense fruit flavour than is found in other raspberry vinegars. As a result, you can use it more sparingly. Add a hint of mint by including several sprigs of fresh mint with the raspberries.

2 cups	raspberries, fresh or frozen and thawed	500 mL
1¼ cups	red wine vinegar	300 mL
⅓ cup	granulated sugar	75 mL
¼ cup	water	50 mL

1. Place raspberries, vinegar, sugar and water in a medium stainless steel or enamel saucepan. Bring to a boil over high heat, reduce heat, cover and boil gently for 5 minutes. Cool before storing; store in the refrigerator overnight.
2. Strain through a fine sieve, pressing to extract liquid; discard pulp. Pour liquid into a clean jar with a tight-fitting lid. Store in the refrigerator.

Makes 2 cups (500 mL).

Herbed Lemon Vinegar

We love the fresh flavour of this lemon vinegar. Splash it lightly on fish before baking or use it instead of butter with cooked vegetables. We also use it in a vinaigrette for a fruit salad. Garlic lovers will certainly want to include the garlic!

2	lemons	2
2 cups	white wine vinegar	500 mL
1 tbsp	dried dill weed, basil, rosemary or	15 mL
	tarragon *or* 4 small sprigs fresh herbs	
2	cloves garlic, sliced, optional	2
2 tsp	granulated sugar	10 mL

1. Finely grate outside rind of lemons and thinly slice lemons. Combine rind, lemon slices, vinegar, herbs and garlic (if using) in a medium stainless steel or enamel saucepan. Bring to a boil over high heat, remove from heat and let cool.
2. Pour into a clean jar. Cover and steep in a cool dark place for several weeks. Taste vinegar occasionally and when strength is satisfactory, strain vinegar and discard pulp. Heat vinegar with sugar until sugar is dissolved; pour into a clean jar with a tight-fitting lid. Store in the refrigerator.

Makes about 2 cups (500 mL).

Vinaigrettes and Dressings

Now that we have talked about specialty vinegars and flavoured oils, here are some of our favourite ways to use them. See Chapter 14 for others.

Light Garlic-Basil Vinaigrette

Use this dressing on a salad of tossed greens or mesclun, to marinate meats or to sprinkle on steamed vegetables for a vegetable salad.

¼ cup	chicken broth	50 mL
3 tbsp	Basil Oil with Lemon and Black Peppercorns (page 176)	45 mL
1 tbsp	red wine vinegar	15 mL
2 tsp	lemon juice	10 mL
1 tsp	Dijon-Style Mustard (page 166)	5 mL
1	clove garlic, crushed	1
1 tbsp	chopped fresh basil or 1 tsp (5 mL) dried	15 mL

Combine all ingredients in a small container with a tight-fitting lid. Cover and shake well. Refrigerate until ready to use.

Makes ½ cup (125 mL).

Oregano Pepper Vinaigrette

This is a robust vinaigrette. It delivers zip to many an ordinary green salad. Drizzle some on sliced tomatoes. We like it with a pasta salad.

⅓ cup	Five-Pepper Oil (page 178)	75 mL
¼ cup	dry red wine	45 mL
1 tbsp	chopped fresh oregano or	15 mL
	1 tsp (5 mL) dried	
1 tbsp	red wine vinegar	15 mL
1	clove garlic, crushed	1
¼ tsp	salt	1 mL

Combine all ingredients in a small container with a tight-fitting lid. Cover and shake well. Refrigerate until ready to use.

Makes about ½ cup (125 mL).

Greek Salad
Place 8 cups (2 L) torn romaine lettuce, ½ red onion and ½ English cucumber, thinly sliced, ¼ cup pitted kalamata olives, 2 medium tomatoes cut into wedges and ½ cup (125 mL) crumbled feta cheese in a large bowl. Pour Oregano Pepper Vinaigrette over salad; toss well. Makes 8 servings.

Raspberry Orange Vinaigrette

This is the perfect vinaigrette to use with fruit salads and with cottage cheese salads. And use it as a marinade for chicken and pork before grilling.

⅓ cup	orange juice	75 mL
¼ cup	each: extra virgin olive oil and water	50 mL
2 tbsp	Red Wine Raspberry Vinegar (page 181)	25 mL
1	chopped green onion	1
⅛ tsp	each: salt and freshly ground pepper	0.5 mL

Combine all ingredients in a small container with a tight-fitting lid. Cover and shake well. Refrigerate until ready to use.

Makes ⅔ cup (150 mL).

Creamy Champagne Dressing

You don't need to wait for a special day to make this flavourful dressing using our Champagne Vinegar. Use it for salads of shredded cabbage, chopped celery and diced apple, or for a light potato salad.

3 tbsp	light mayonnaise	45 mL
3 tbsp	Champagne Vinegar (page 180)	45 mL
2 tbsp	canola oil	25 mL
1 tbsp	chopped fresh parsley	15 mL
1 tbsp	water	15 mL
1 tsp	Old-Style Whole Seed Mustard (page 169) or coarse mustard	5 mL

Whisk together mayonnaise, vinegar, oil, parsley, water and mustard in a small bowl. Transfer to a container with a tight-fitting lid. Cover and refrigerate until ready to use.

Makes about ½ cup (125 mL).

Tip:

Mesclun

Today there is much consumer interest in a variety of lettuces usually called mesclun or mixed young salad greens. They are available in almost every produce store and supermarket, sold by weight. Typically they are a combination of mild- and bitter-flavoured tender young leaves of different colours. The combination usually includes oak leaf and red leaf lettuces, frisée (curly endive), mâche and radicchio, and may include spinach, red mustard, arugula and others. Store as you would other greens and use as soon as possible, ideally within a couple of days.

Chapter Twelve

The Finishing Touch

T HIS IS A CHAPTER of wonderful "finishing" ideas. Not all of them are completed desserts, but all are used in some way in the dessert part of the meal. For example, Raspberry Coulis and Hazelnut Fudge Sauce (pages 191 and 194) are luscious ideas for topping something else like ice cream, cake, fresh fruit or pudding. But you may still be tempted to eat them with a spoon directly from the jar. Our Pear and Sour Cherry Mincemeat and Traditional Rumtopf (pages 188 and 189) are other topping ideas.

Most of our finishing ideas, once prepared with a lid on them, are then available for fast dessert delivery at a moment's notice.

And then there are the liqueurs. They are not really desserts, but are used to accompany after-dessert coffee. We offer you three fresh-tasting fruit liqueurs and two creamy ones. The fruit liqueurs can also be used as dessert toppings, but the creamy ones are best with coffee.

We believe our finishing touch ideas are well worth your preparation time and will meet your needs for fast-start desserts.

Serving Suggestions

Add Candied Fruits (page 195) to cakes, muffins and squares. Keep Brandied Butterscotch Sauce (page 194) on hand to serve as a tasty dip for apple slices. Fruit Liqueurs (pages 198–199) added to chilled soda water or white wine make wonderful spritzers.

List of Recipes

Pear and Sour Cherry Mincemeat

For many years making mincemeat has been a tradition in our families. Lighter in colour and flavour than traditional mincemeat, this pear version has wider uses than just for pies and tarts. Try it as a topping for pound cake, ice cream, and waffles or pancakes. Or use it in place of date filling in your favourite date square recipe. Sour cherries or cranberries add colour and just a hint of tartness.

4	Bartlett pears, peeled, cored and finely chopped	4
1 cup	golden raisins	250 mL
½	orange, chopped (include rind as well as pulp)	½
½ cup	chopped sour cherries or cranberries	125 mL
¾ cup	packed brown sugar	175 mL
¼ cup	water	50 mL
	Grated rind and juice of 1 lemon	
½ tsp	each: ground cinnamon and allspice	2 mL
¼ tsp	ground nutmeg	1 mL
2 tbsp	brandy	25 mL

1. Combine pears, raisins, orange, cherries, sugar, water, lemon rind and juice, cinnamon, allspice and nutmeg in a medium stainless steel or enamel saucepan. Bring to a boil over high heat, reduce heat, cover and boil gently for 20 minutes or until thickened, stirring frequently. Stir in brandy and return to a boil.
2. Remove hot jars from canner and ladle mincemeat into jars to within ½ inch (1 cm) of rim (head space). Process for 20 minutes for half-pint (250 mL) and pint (500 mL) jars as directed on page 93 (Longer Time Processing Procedure).

Makes 2¾ cups (675 mL).

Turn to page 119 for a delicious caponata
to serve on toasted baguette slices.

Traditional Rumtopf

Rumtopf comes from the German word *Topf*, meaning "pot." The traditional version is made in a large crock, different fruits added as they ripen during the growing season. If you don't have a crock, simply layer the fruit in either a very large glass jar or a large non-reactive container.

1½ cups	strawberries, whole or halved if large	375 mL
½ cup	granulated sugar	125 mL
¾ cup	light rum	175 mL

Add ¾ cup (175 mL) of any or all of the following:
red currants, pitted sweet cherries, raspberries, blueberries, sliced peaches, sliced nectarines, quartered apricots, quartered blue or yellow plums

Granulated sugar
Rum

1. Place strawberries into an 8-cup (2-L) container and layer with sugar. Allow to stand for 30 minutes. Slowly pour rum down inside of jar so it measures about 2 inches (5 cm) over fruit. Cover loosely with plastic film. Store in a cool location (basement or a cool room) for about 2 weeks (see Tip).
2. Combine next choice of fruit and ¼ cup (50 mL) sugar; add to contents of jar. Top up with rum, if required, so fruit is covered with liquid. Since the fruit has tendency to float, place a small plate or other non-reactive item on top of the fruit to keep it submerged. Otherwise stir every few days.
3. Repeat with other fruits as they are available. With each addition, add ¼ cup (50 mL) sugar and top up with rum if required.
4. When fermentation is complete, fruit is no longer bubbling; transfer fruit to clean jars with tight-fitting lids. Store in the refrigerator.

Makes 6 to 12 cups (1.5 to 3 L) depending on how many fruits you use.

Chunky Basil Pasta Sauce (page 155),
Roasted Vegetable Pasta Sauce (page 156),
and Seasoned Tomato Sauce (page 158)
are a few of the savoury sauces featured in
Chapter Ten.

Fruit Toppings and Sauces

These exceptional fruit sauces turn plain cake, waffles, French toast, ice cream and frozen yogurt into elegant desserts at a moment's notice. Tucked in your freezer, they are great to have on hand.

Slow-Baked Apple Wedges

Slow baking transforms apples into rich golden wedges. Wonderful with a spice cake!

¾ cup	liquid honey	175 mL
½ cup	water	125 mL
3 tbsp	lemon juice	45 mL
⅛ tsp	ground nutmeg	0.5 mL
8	large tart apples, peeled and cut into thick wedges	8

1. Combine honey, water, lemon juice and nutmeg in a large bowl. Add apple wedges, stirring to coat well.
2. Spread apples in a 10 x 15 inch (24 x 40 cm) jelly roll pan, pouring any remaining liquid over top. Cover with foil and bake at 300°F (150°C) for 45 minutes or until apples are soft. Remove foil and bake until apples are golden and most of liquid has evaporated, about 75 minutes (50 minutes in a convection oven). Using a flat lifter, gently turn apples once or twice during baking.
3. Pack into clean jars or plastic containers to within ½ inch (1 cm) of rim. Cover with tight-fitting lids. Store in refrigerator for up to 1 week or freeze for longer storage.

Makes 3 cups (750 mL).

Peach Slices with Maple Syrup

This is a wonderful topping to make when peaches are at their most flavourful.

½ cup	pure maple syrup	125 mL
¼ cup	granulated sugar	50 mL
2 tbsp	sherry, optional	25 mL
6	large peaches, peeled and sliced	6

1. Combine syrup and sugar in a 4-cup (1-L) microwavable container. Micro-wave at High (100%) for 1½ minutes or until sugar is dissolved. Stir in sherry, if using.
2. Add peach slices, cover and microwave for 5 minutes or just until mixture begins to boil. Cool, stirring occasionally.
3. Pack into clean jars or plastic containers to within ½ inch (1 cm) of rim. Cover with tight-fitting lids. Store in refrigerator for up to 1 week or freeze for longer storage.

Makes about 3 cups (750 mL).

Raspberry Coulis

Raspberry coulis has a myriad of uses, both as a topping for crêpes or pancakes and with an elegant dessert such as a frozen cream mousse or over waffles.

4 cups	fresh raspberries	1 L
½ cup	icing sugar	125 mL
1 tbsp	orange liqueur, optional	15 mL

1. Purée raspberries in a food processor or blender. Stir in sugar and liqueur and press through a medium sieve to remove seeds.
2. Pack into clean jars or plastic containers to within ½ inch (1 cm) of rim. Cover with tight-fitting lids. Store in refrigerator for up to 3 weeks or freeze for longer storage.

Makes 1¾ cups (425 mL).

Piquant Sour Cherry Sauce

This bright flavourful sauce always brings requests for the recipe. If you prefer it less piquant, add a bit of extra sugar.

4½ cups	fresh or frozen pitted sour cherries	1.125 L
1½ cups	water	375 mL
¾ cup	pineapple juice	175 mL
1	cinnamon stick, 4 inches (10 cm) long	1
¾ cup	granulated sugar	175 mL
3 tbsp	cornstarch	45 mL
⅓ cup	cold water	75 mL
2 tbsp	lemon juice	25 mL

1. Combine cherries, water, pineapple juice and cinnamon stick in a medium stainless steel or enamel saucepan. Bring to a boil over high heat, reduce heat, cover and boil gently for 10 minutes. Remove cinnamon and discard.
2. Add sugar to cherries. Blend together cornstarch and water and stir into cherries. Return to a boil, reduce heat and boil gently, uncovered, for 5 minutes or until clear and thickened. Stir in lemon juice.
3. Pack into clean jars or plastic containers to within ½ inch (1 cm) of rim. Cover with tight-fitting lids. Store in refrigerator for up to 3 weeks or freeze for longer storage.

Makes about 2¼ cups (550 mL).

Strawberry Smooch

Bernardin Canada shared this recipe with us for a fresh-tasting berry sauce. They suggest serving it over pancakes and waffles, frozen desserts or fruit salad, or over or under cake. You could also use it to sweeten and add flavour to cereals. Using a powdered fruit pectin provides the thicker consistency you expect from a fruit sauce.

7 cups	halved or quartered strawberries	1.75 L
1½ cups	maple syrup	375 mL
1 cup	unsweetened apple juice	250 mL
3 tbsp	lemon juice	45 mL
1	pkg (57 g) powdered fruit pectin	1

1. Purée strawberries in a blender or food processor. You should have 4¾ cups (1.175 L) puréed fruit. Place in a large stainless steel or enamel saucepan.
2. Add maple syrup, apple juice and lemon juice. Bring to a boil over medium-high heat. Gradually stir pectin into fruit. Return mixture to a full boil for 1 minute, stirring constantly. Remove from heat.
3. Pour fruit into hot jars and fill with syrup to within ½ inch (1 cm) of rim (head space). Process 10 minutes for half-pint (250 mL) jars as directed on page 93 (Longer Time Processing Procedure).

Makes 6 half-pint (250 mL) jars.

Rich Dessert Sauces

We like to keep several of these sauces in the refrigerator. They make wonderful quick toppings for puddings, fresh fruit, crêpes, pound cake, angel food cake or ice cream. You can also serve them under cream puffs or as a dessert fondue sauce.

Mocha Caramel Sauce

This is an exquisite chocolate sauce graced with a hint of caramel and coffee.

½ cup	granulated sugar	125 mL
3 tbsp	water	45 mL
¼ cup	espresso or very strong coffee	50 mL
2 tbsp	corn syrup	25 mL
2 tbsp	butter	25 mL
½ cup	10% cream	125 mL
3	squares semi-sweet chocolate	3
½ tsp	vanilla extract	2 mL

1. Combine sugar and water in a heavy medium saucepan. Bring to a boil over medium-high heat, stirring just until sugar is dissolved. Swirl pan slightly to dissolve any sugar crystals on sides. Continue to boil gently without stirring until sugar turns a rich golden caramel colour, about 7 minutes. Watch carefully toward the end of the cooking time as it will burn very quickly.
2. Remove from heat and carefully pour in coffee, stirring well until all the caramel is dissolved. Stir in corn syrup and butter; return to heat and bring just to a boil, stirring constantly. Remove from heat.
3. Pour hot mixture slowly into cream; blend in chocolate and vanilla. Pour into a clean jar with a tight-fitting lid. Store in refrigerator for up to 1 month. Serve slightly warmed.

Makes 1¼ cups (325 mL).

Brandied Butterscotch Sauce

This sauce's authentic butterscotch flavour and hint of brandy make it a wonderful dip for apple slices.

⅔ cup	lightly packed brown sugar	150 mL
⅓ cup	butter	75 mL
¼ cup	corn syrup	50 mL
½ cup	18% cream	125 mL
2 tbsp	brandy	25 mL
1 tsp	vanilla extract	5 mL

1. Combine sugar, butter and corn syrup in a small saucepan. Bring to a boil, over high heat, stirring frequently; reduce heat to medium and boil gently for 3 minutes. Remove from heat.
2. Cool for 5 minutes; stir in cream, brandy and vanilla. Pour into a clean jar with a tight-fitting lid. Store in refrigerator for up to 3 weeks. Stir before serving.

Makes 1½ cups (375 mL).

Hazelnut Fudge Sauce

This rich chocolate sauce brims with the taste of toasted hazelnuts.

¼ cup	butter	50 mL
½ cup	coarsely chopped hazelnuts	125 mL
1 cup	granulated sugar	250 mL
½ cup	cocoa	125 mL
⅛ tsp	salt	0.5 mL
⅓ cup	corn syrup	75 mL
¾ cup	10% cream	175 mL
½ tsp	vanilla extract	2 mL

1. Melt butter in a medium saucepan over medium heat. Add nuts and sauté for 5 minutes or until lightly browned. Remove from heat.
2. Stir in sugar, cocoa and salt. Blend in corn syrup, mixing well; stir in cream. Return to medium heat and boil gently for 1 minute, stirring constantly. Remove from heat and stir in vanilla.
3. Pour into a clean jar with a tight-fitting lid. Store in refrigerator for up to 3 weeks.

Makes 2 cups (500 mL).

Candied Fruits

Dried fruits have many uses. Serve them as a sweet treat for nibbling, add them to baking or stir them into frozen desserts.

Dried Cranberries

Commercial dried cranberries are expensive and their availability is unreliable. However, fresh cranberries can be dried at home using our simple method. Keep them on hand to add flavour and colour to muffins, squares and holiday baking. They turn plain cooked oatmeal into a breakfast treat.

2 cups	fresh cranberries	500 mL
¼ cup	granulated sugar	50 mL

1. Cut cranberries in half and place in a medium bowl; mix in sugar. Cover and let stand for 24 hours, stirring occasionally. Drain off liquid.
2. Place cranberries on a baking sheet and place in a 100°F (38°C) oven for 4 hours or until berries are almost dry. Remove from oven and leave on baking sheet at room temperature to air-dry for 24 hours.
3. Pack in an airtight container and store in the refrigerator up to 1 month or freeze for longer storage.

Makes ¾ cup (175 mL).

Candied Ginger

Candied ginger, often called crystallized ginger, is a spirited addition to a candy tray and a pleasant compliment to chocolate. Its lively flavour is a nice addition to a variety of baked products. Remember to make extra for gifts during the holidays. We have used it in many of our other recipes throughout the book.

1 cup	thinly sliced peeled gingerroot	250 mL
	Cold water for boiling	
¾ cup	water	175 mL
½ cup	granulated sugar	125 mL
	Extra granulated sugar for coating	

1. Place ginger in a small saucepan and cover with cold water. Bring to a boil over high heat, reduce heat, cover and boil gently for 15 minutes. Drain and repeat process with fresh cold water.
2. Combine ginger, ¾ cup (175 mL) water and sugar in a saucepan. Bring to a boil over high heat, reduce heat and boil gently, uncovered, for about 30 minutes or until liquid is evaporated completely. Watch carefully during last 10 minutes to prevent scorching.
3. Put extra sugar in a flat dish about ¼ inch (1 cm) thick. Remove a few pieces of ginger with a fork and toss them in sugar to coat both sides; place on a cooling rack set on a baking pan. Repeat until all slices are done. Dry in a 200°F (93°C) oven for 1 hour or until ginger feels soft and no longer sticky. Let stand at room temperature for 1 day to finish drying.
4. Place slices in an airtight container and store in the refrigerator.

Makes 1 cup (250 mL).

Candied Citrus Peel

A zesty treat on its own, candied peel is also a nice addition to many desserts and baked products. For special occasions, dip candied peel in chocolate.

	Rind from 2 grapefruit, or 3 sweet or	
	blood oranges, or 3 lemons, or	
	a mixture of all three	
	Cold water	
¾ cup	granulated sugar	175 mL
¾ cup	water	175 mL
½ tbsp	corn syrup	7 mL
	Extra granulated sugar, about	
	½ cup (125 mL)	

1. Cut fruit in quarters lengthwise. Remove the rind from pulp; save pulp for another use. Slice rinds into ½-inch (1-cm) slices. You should have about 2 cups (500 mL).
2. Place rinds in a medium saucepan and cover with cold water. Bring to a boil over high heat, reduce heat and boil gently for 2 minutes or longer if you do not like the strong citrus flavour (see Tip). Drain well.
3. Combine sugar, ¾ cup (175 mL) water and corn syrup in pan and bring to a boil over high heat. Add rinds, return to boil, cover and boil gently for 15 minutes. Remove cover and continue to boil gently for about 30 minutes or until liquid is reduced to about 2 tablespoons (25 mL). Remove rinds to a cooling rack to drain.
4. When rinds are well drained, roll a few at a time in extra sugar, being careful to coat well. Place on a baking sheet or wax paper. Repeat until all are done. Let sit at room temperature to air-dry for 24 hours.
5. Pack in airtight containers and store in the refrigerator.

Makes 2 cups (500 mL).

Tip: If you are using lemon rinds, cook them first for 15 minutes before adding remaining rinds; cook 2 minutes longer.

Liqueurs

All of these liqueurs may be stored in the refrigerator for several months to enjoy at your leisure.

Cranberry Orange Liqueur

Ruby-red cranberry and orange liqueur has a smooth and pleasingly tart taste. It is wonderful "on the rocks" or served as a spritzer with chilled soda water.

3 cups	cranberry juice	750 mL
½ cup	orange juice concentrate, thawed	125 mL
½ cup	granulated sugar	125 mL
1 cup	vodka	250 mL
½ tsp	vanilla extract	2 mL

1. Combine cranberry cocktail, orange juice and sugar in a medium saucepan. Bring to a boil over medium–high heat, stirring until sugar is dissolved. Reduce heat and boil gently, uncovered, for about 10 minutes or until reduced by half. Remove from heat.
2. Cool to room temperature, stir in vodka and vanilla. Pour into a clean jar with a tight-fitting lid. Store in the refrigerator.

Makes about 3 cups (750 mL).

Tipsy Fruit Topping
A simple elegant topping for pound or angel food cake, ice cream or fresh seasonal fruit.
Combine 1 cup (250 mL) each orange and pineapple juice, ½ cup (125 mL) granulated sugar and a cinnamon stick in a large shallow skillet. Bring to a boil, reduce heat and boil gently for 5 minutes. Add sliced peeled pears, peaches or nectarines, and boil gently 5 minutes or until fruit is tender. Remove from heat and add ¼ cup (50 mL) of your choice of fruit liqueur. Serve warm or chilled.

Framboise

More commonly known as a raspberry liqueur, our Framboise is quickly made using frozen raspberry concentrate, orange juice and some brandy or vodka. It is delicious served over ice with sparkling mineral water.

1	can (12 oz/341 mL) frozen undiluted raspberry cocktail, thawed	1
1 cup	vodka or brandy	250 mL
½ cup	granulated sugar	125 mL
3 tbsp	orange juice concentrate	45 mL

1. Place raspberry cocktail, vodka, sugar and orange juice in a clean jar with a tight-fitting lid. Seal tightly and shake until sugar is blended.
2. Let stand at room temperature for at least 2 weeks for flavours to blend. Shake jar occasionally. When ready to use, store in the refrigerator.

Makes 2½ cups (625 mL).

Apricot Brandy

Not only does this simple recipe make an exquisite brandy, but the reserved apricots are also positively heavenly served over ice cream.

1 cup	dried apricots, coarsely chopped, about 6 oz (170 g)	250 mL
1½ cups	dry white wine	375 mL
¾ cup	granulated sugar	175 mL
1 cup	brandy	250 mL

1. Place apricots, wine and sugar in a small microwavable container. Microwave at High (100%) for 4 to 6 minutes or until sugar is dissolved and mixture comes to a boil. Cool to room temperature.
2. Pour into a clean quart (1 L) jar with a tight-fitting lid. Add brandy, seal and let stand in a cool dark place for 1 month. Shake bottle occasionally. Strain through a fine sieve lined with several layers of cheesecloth. Reserve the apricots for another use.

Makes 2¼ cups (550 mL)

Liqueurs for Coffee

Pair one of these easily made liqueurs with freshly brewed coffee for a luxurious finish to a good meal. Both have an alcohol content of approximately 15% so they will keep in the refrigerator for up to 2 months. Use one half of the base for each liqueur recipe.

Liqueur Base

| 2 cups | 18% cream | 500 mL |
| 1 | can (300 mL) sweetened condensed milk | 1 |

Whisk cream and milk together until well blended. Divide into 2 equal parts of 1⅔ cups (400 mL) each. Use 1 part to make each recipe below or make a double recipe of your favourite.

Irish Isles Cream

Irish Isles Cream is an affordable simulation of the famous Irish Cream. Use rye whisky for a Canadian version. Miniature bottles of coconut rum are available in most liquor stores.
Combine 1⅔ cups (400 mL) Liqueur Base, 1 cup (250 mL) Irish whisky, ¼ cup (50 mL) coconut rum or ½ tsp (2 mL) coconut extract, 1 tbsp (15 mL) chocolate drink syrup and 1 tsp (5 mL) vanilla extract. Pour into a clean bottle with a tight-fitting lid. Store in refrigerator for up to 2 months. Makes 3 cups (750 mL).

Spanish Cream

Spanish Cream combines the requisite liqueurs for Spanish Coffee in a convenient ready-to-use form.
Combine 1⅔ cups (400 mL) Liqueur Base, ¾ cup (175 mL) brandy, ½ cup (125 mL) coffee liqueur and ¼ cup (50 mL) Triple Sec. Pour into a clean bottle with a tight-fitting lid. Store in refrigerator for up to 2 months. Makes 3 cups (750 mL).

Chapter Thirteen

Baby and Kid Food

A T SOME TIME in our lives, many of us have a very special group of people to cater to ... our children. From the time they leave their mother's breast (or their bottle of formula), we have the wonderful responsibility to nurture their young bodies—and taste buds—with healthy nutritious food. As they grow, we have the challenging opportunity to further encourage our children in healthy eating habits that will benefit them for their entire lives. And many children will develop a lifelong interest in cooking nutritious and tasty food themselves from their early food experiences. All of this is certainly worth "Putting a Lid on It" for the next generation.

List of Recipes

Baby Food

You don't have to buy special baby food for your baby or toddler. With the help of a blender or food processor, it is easy to prepare your own using fresh nutritional foods.

Choosing Foods

Freshly picked vegetables and fruits have not yet lost their nutrients and so are the best choice. At other times of the year, use frozen foods without sauce or seasonings. Fruits canned in their own juices with no added sugar are also a good choice. Canned vegetables are not appropriate as they generally contain added salt.

Purée fresh or frozen lean meat and fish to a consistency your baby or toddler will enjoy. Look for low-fat cuts and avoid processed meats of all kinds such as sausage, bacon or bologna.

Baby Food Suggestions

Whatever you prepare, keep foods simple and let baby or toddler savour the original taste of freshly prepared nutritious food. It's the start of a healthy lifetime preference.

- Cooked fruits such as apples, apricots, peaches, pears, plums or prunes.
- Mashed raw, ripe bananas, papayas or mangoes.
- Cooked young tender vegetables such as asparagus, beets, broccoli, carrots, cauliflower, green beans, peas, sweet potatoes, and both summer and winter squash.
- Cooked cubes of boneless skinless chicken or turkey breast, lean beef, or fish such as sole, halibut, haddock or salmon.
- A simple stew of lean beef or chicken cubes, mixed with potato. As the baby becomes used to a mixture of foods, add other vegetables. When preparing food for the whole family, be sure to remove the baby's portion first before adding salt, spices or sugar.

Preparing Baby Food

1. Before you begin, make sure your hands and all food preparation surfaces are clean.
2. Peel vegetables and fruits if required and cook using as little water as possible, just until they are tender to prevent loss of nutrients. Either boil in a small covered saucepan with about ¼ inch (0.5 cm) water in the bottom or microwave, covered, with a sprinkling of water. Vegetables may also be steamed using a rack over boiling water.
3. The easy and practical method for cooking meats is to microwave them at Medium (50%). Other good ways are to simmer the meat in a small amount of water or wrap it tightly in aluminum foil and bake in a 325°F (160°C) oven. The tight seal retains the moisture and the slow moist heat will soften the tough fibres in the meat. Reserve all cooking liquid for making the purée.
4. After the food is cooked, place small pieces in the container of a blender or food processor. Add enough of the cooking liquid, water, fruit juice, milk or formula to make a smooth purée. Most blenders work best with smaller amounts of food, so process in several batches if you are preparing a large quantity.
5. When baby food is the right consistency, place it in a small jar, cover and cool quickly in the refrigerator. The rule for food safety is never leave food standing at room temperature.
6. Avoid adding salt, spices and sugar to baby food. Baby taste buds are much more sensitive to these additives than are adults, and baby kidneys cannot excrete surplus salt. The best food is the freshest you can find, with nothing added.
7. Freshly prepared food can be stored in the refrigerator for up to 2 days. Save time by making larger batches, then freezing or processing for longer storage

Freezing Baby Food

The easiest way to keep the prepared food is to freeze it if you plan to keep it longer than 2 days.

1. Freezing the food in ice cube trays allows you to remove just the right amount for tiny appetites. There are no leftovers and no storage problems. When the cubes are frozen, usually after 8 to 12 hours, pop them out of the tray and place in plastic freezer bags. If you use small freezer containers, allow about 1 inch (2.5 cm) head space in the container and make sure the lid fits tightly.

2. Label and date everything. You may think you'll remember what is in the container, but freezing has the annoying habit of making foods look much the same.

3. It is important to put the food in the freezer immediately after preparation. Never allow it to stand at room temperature.

4. Use the frozen food within 6 to 8 weeks. It dries out during more extended frozen storage and loses nutritional value. If you find the baby food is a bit dry, add extra liquid such as milk or broth when you reheat it.

5. At mealtime, heat the frozen food in small heat-proof dishes at Low (30%) in the microwave. Do not heat in the plastic storage containers. Heating can also be done on a stove top in small dishes placed in a skillet filled with about 1 inch (2.5 cm) of water. Whatever the heating method, be sure to stir the food before serving to distribute the heat and test for temperature before feeding it to your child.

Processing Fruit Purées

A purée of fresh fruit may be safely processed in a boiling-water canner. The small ½-cup (125-mL) or 1-cup (250-mL) jars are a convenient size for a small appetites to eat within 2 days. Vegetables, fish and meat are not suitable for preserving by boiling water since they require higher temperatures than those reached by boiling water. Unless you have a pressure canner, these foods must be frozen for longer storage.

1. Wash fruit, peel if desired and remove pit, seeds and stems. Measure cut-up fruit into a large stainless steel or enamel saucepan and add 1 cup (250 mL) water for every 4 cups (1 L) fruit. Bring to a boil over medium-high heat, stirring frequently. Reduce heat, cover and boil gently until fruit is very soft, about 10 to 20 minutes.

2. Pour fruit and liquid into a blender or food-processor container and process until smooth; or press through a food mill.

3. Remove jars from canner and ladle purée into hot jars to within ½ inch (1 cm) of top rim (head space). Process for 20 minutes for quarter-pint (125-mL) and half-pint (250-mL) jars as directed on page 93 (Longer Time Processing Procedure).

Kid Food

Kids love to make their own foods. Let them try the following recipes ... or any others that are suitably simple for young beginning cooks. It could be the first step to a lifelong interest in cooking. Of course, make sure there's an adult nearby whenever children use a stove or barbecue!

Sweet Pickled Anything

Choose from a variety of vegetables to make your very own pickles.

Vegetables

5 cups	Choose several of the following:	1.25 mL
	Asparagus, tough ends removed	
	Carrots, peeled and cut into chunks or strips	
	Cauliflower, cut into small pieces	
	Broccoli, cut into small pieces	
	Yellow wax beans, ends trimmed	
	Tiny onions, peeled	
	Baby corn cobs, husked	
	Sweet red, green or yellow peppers, halved, seeds removed and cut into squares or strips	
	Snow peas, ends trimmed	
	Zucchini, cut into chunks or strips	

Pickling Syrup

2 cups	cider or white vinegar	500 mL
1 cup	granulated sugar	250 mL
½ cup	water	125 mL
½ tsp	pickling salt	2 mL
2 tsp	Choose one of the following spices:	10 mL
	Pickling spice	
	Cinnamon sticks	
	Whole cloves	
	Whole allspice berries	
	Mustard seeds	
	Dill seeds	

To Cook Vegetables:

1. Wash the vegetables you are using and cut into large pieces.
2. Bring another large pot of water to a boil on top of the stove. When the water starts to boil, put the prepared vegetables into the boiling water and cook them about 2 minutes or until they are just slightly tender when you insert the point of a sharp knife.

   Note: Pickled foods should be crisp—be sure you don't cook the vegetables too much. Vegetables such as onions, carrots and cauliflower require longer cooking, so put them into the water first. Vegetables such as zucchini require very little cooking, so add them a few minutes later, and snow peas don't require any cooking. Have a large strainer ready in the sink to pour the vegetables into when they are finished cooking.
3. Pour the cooked vegetables into the strainer to allow the hot water to drain off and then pour cold water over the vegetables.

To Make Pickling Syrup:

Combine vinegar, sugar, water and salt in a large saucepan. Add the spices you want to use to flavour your pickled foods and bring mixture to a boil over high heat. Reduce heat and simmer for 5 minutes.

To Process Pickles:

1. Wash 2 pint (500 mL) mason jars to hold the pickled foods.
2. Partially fill a boiling-water canner with hot water. Place the clean mason jars in canner, cover and begin to bring water to a boil over high heat.
3. Place the snap lids in boiling water for 5 minutes before you are ready to fill the jars. Follow the manufacturer's directions on the package.
4. Remove the hot jars from the canner with tongs and pack the cooked vegetables into the jars. A wide-mouth funnel helps get the vegetables into the jar. Carefully pour the pickling syrup into the jars to within ½ inch (1 cm) of top rim (head space). Allow some of the spices to go into the jar or remove them, depending on how spicy you want your pickled foods.
5. Remove air bubbles from inside the jars by sliding a clean small wooden or plastic spatula between glass and food; add more syrup if needed to adjust the head space to ½ inch (1 cm). Wipe jar rim to remove any stickiness. Centre the snap lid on jar; apply screw band just until fingertip tight. Place jars in canner and adjust water level to cover jars by 1 inch (2.5 cm). Cover canner and return water to a boil. When the water is boiling, set the timer and process for 10 minutes for pint (500 mL) jars.
6. Remove jars from canner and cool for 24 hours. Check jar seals (sealed lids turn downward). Remove screw bands, dry and either replace loosely on jar or store separately. Wipe jars and make labels for your very own pickles. Store the pickled foods in a cool dark place for at least 2 weeks before tasting them.

Makes 2 pint (500 mL) jars.

Chunky Applesauce

Given a bit of help with the apple peeling, kids can have fun making applesauce spiced with dried fruit.

5 lb	tart firm apples (about 20 apples)	2.5 kg
⅓ cup	water	75 mL
¼ cup	dried fruit such as cherries, cranberries, raisins or chopped apricots	50 mL
½ cup	granulated sugar *or* honey	125 mL

1. Peel apples and remove core. Cut into large chunks and place in a large sauce-pan. Add water and bring to a boil over high heat, reduce heat, cover and sim-mer until apples are tender, about 10 to 20 minutes. Stir occasionally.
2. Meanwhile, partially fill a boiling-water canner with hot water. Place 3 clean pint (500 mL) jars in canner, cover and begin to bring water to a boil over high heat.
3. Add dried fruit to apples and stir in sugar or honey. Add more to make a slightly sweet sauce.
4. Meanwhile, place snap lids in boiling water according to directions on the package.
5. Remove jars from canner and ladle applesauce into hot jars to within ½ inch (1 cm) of top rim (head space). Remove air bubbles by sliding a clean small wooden or plastic spatula between glass and food; readjust the head space to ½ inch (1 cm). Wipe jar rim to remove any stickiness. Centre snap lid on jar; apply screw band just until fingertip tight.
6. Place jars in canner and adjust water level to cover jars by 1 inch (2.5 cm). Cover canner and return water to boil. Process for 20 minutes for pint (500 mL) jars.
7. Remove jars from canner to a surface covered with newspapers or with several layers of paper towels and cool for 24 hours. Check jar seals (sealed lids turn downward). Remove screw bands, dry and either replace loosely on jar or store separately. Wipe jars, label with contents and date and store in a cool, dark place.

Makes 3 pint (500 mL) jars.

Frozen Pops

Make these easy treats to enjoy with your family or friends on a hot day.

Sunny Gold Pops

Margaret's granddaughter, Chelsea, made and served this refreshing frozen treat to her friend Sarah. They both came back for seconds.

1	can (6 oz/170 mL) frozen orange juice concentrate, thawed	1
1 cup	milk	250 mL
½ cup	each: pineapple juice and water	125 mL
¼ cup	liquid honey	50 mL
1 tsp	vanilla extract	5 mL
10	ice cubes	10

Combine orange juice, milk, pineapple juice, water, honey, vanilla and ice cubes in a blender container. Process with on/off motion until smooth. To freeze pops, see below. Makes 6 large pops or 4 cups (1 L).

Fruit Yogurt Pops

Another hit, this one is absolutely "kid perfect."

3 cups	chopped fresh fruit, such as strawberries, raspberries, peaches, nectarines, mangoes or bananas (see Tip)	750 mL
2 cups	plain yogurt	500 mL
¾ cup	fruit jam or icing sugar	175 mL

Finely chop fruit in a food processor or blender or mash soft fruits with a fork or potato masher. Stir in yogurt and jam or sugar, mixing well. To freeze pops, see below. Makes about 6 large pops or 4 cups (1 L).

> **Tip:** Use 1 pkg (425 g) frozen strawberries, raspberries or peaches in place of fresh fruit and reduce sugar to ½ cup (125 mL) if desired.

To Freeze Pops:
1. Place paper cups or popsicle moulds in a flat pan. Divide fruit mixture evenly among the cups. Insert a stick into each and freeze until firm.
2. Remove cups from freezer 15 minutes before serving or place in a microwave oven on defrost for 1 minute. Peel off paper or remove from popsicle mould and enjoy. Alternatively, pour mixture into a shallow pan and freeze; stir every 30 minutes until frozen to break up ice crystals. Serve in small dishes.

Barbecue Time

Create Your Own Barbecue Sauce

Creative barbecuing is the order of the day. And these barbecue sauces are both creative and still easy enough for children to prepare. Make your own personalized sauce by starting with the Sauce Base and then adding your favourite ingredients. Just remember, something sour, something sweet, something spicy, something neat! Spread your sauce on chicken, pork chops, ribs or hamburgers.

Sauce Base	Something Sour	Something Sweet	Something Spicy
salsa	flavoured vinegar	honey or maple syrup	chile powder
tomato sauce, juice or paste	lemon or lime juice	apple butter	cumin
ketchup	prepared mustard	marmalade	dry mustard
flavoured oil	ginger ale	brown sugar	garlic salt or powder
	tea	jelly	oregano or basil

And now you have something neat!

Create Your Own Berry Cooler

Freeze cubes of berry cooler ahead of time. Then, while your dinner sizzles on the barbecue, make this special summer drink for your friends. You can add extra berries or a sprig of fresh mint for a festive touch.

2 cups	warm water	500 mL
1 cup	granulated sugar	250 mL
2 cups	fresh raspberries or strawberries (see Tip)	500 mL
	Juice of 1 lemon	

1. Combine water and sugar in blender container; use on/off turns to dissolve sugar. Pour half into a large bowl. Add berries and lemon juice to blender; purée until smooth. Pour mixture through a medium sieve to remove seeds. Combine liquid with rest of sugar mixture.
2. Pour into ice cube trays and freeze until firm. Remove cubes from tray, pop them out of the tray and place in plastic freezer bags and return to the freezer.

Makes 3½ cups (875 mL).

To serve:
Fill a glass with frozen juice cubes. Pour in soda water, ginger ale or lemon–lime drink, stirring to dissolve cubes.

Tip: Use a thawed 425 g package frozen berries in place of fresh if desired.

Chapter Fourteen

Let's Open the Lid
and Use What's Inside

WITH OUR pantries full of sparkling jellies, tangy pickles, luscious dessert sauces and zesty savoury sauces, we needed to find ways to use their contents beyond just eating them as is. This sent us back into our kitchens with creative juices at full throttle. The results are in the following pages. We know you will think of many more uses for your preserves, but these will be a start.

We have divided the chapter into recipes and ideas for appetizers, breakfasts, sauces and marinades, vegetables, salads, sandwiches and, naturally, a few favourite sweets, mainly baked items.

We hope you have the same pleasure and satisfaction in your canning and preserving that we have experienced in developing this book. We hope our ideas will help you to turn another meal into a creative dining experience. *Bon appétit!*

List of Recipes

Appetizers

Caramelized Red Onion and Tomato Pizza

Adapted from a Foodland Ontario recipe, this tasty appetizer is easily prepared using our Caramelized Red Onion Relish.

½ cup	Caramelized Red Onion Relish (page 121)	125 mL
4	individual pizza crusts	4
1	medium tomato, diced	1
2 cups	shredded mozzarella cheese	500 mL

Divide onion mixture among pizza crusts, spreading evenly. Combine tomato and cheese; sprinkle over onion. Bake in a 350°F (180°C) oven for about 10 minutes or until hot and cheese is melted. Cut each pizza into 6 wedges.

Makes 24 appetizers.

Italian Cheese and Red Pepper Pizza

Buy an Italian-style flatbread, shred lots of cheese, chop an assortment of vegetables, open a jar of Puttanesco Freezer Pasta Sauce and in minutes you have an appetizer to serve to friends.

1	round Italian-style gourmet flatbread (14 oz/400 g)	1
1½ cups	Puttanesco Freezer Pasta Sauce (page 164)	375 mL
2 cups	shredded Italian cheese (see Tip)	500 mL
1 cup	chopped sweet red peppers	250 mL
½ cup	each: chopped onion and sliced mushrooms	125 mL
¼ cup	grated Parmesan cheese	50 mL
3 tbsp	slivered almonds	45 mL
1 tbsp	chopped fresh oregano or 1 tsp (5 mL) dried	15 mL
2 tsp	chopped fresh basil or 1 tsp (5 mL) dried	10 mL

1. Place flatbread on a large baking pan. Spoon sauce over flatbread, spreading almost to edge. Top with Italian cheese, red pepper, onion, mushrooms, Parmesan cheese, almonds and seasonings.
2. Bake in a 400 °F (200°C) oven for about 15 minutes or until cheese is melted and vegetables are hot. Cut pizza into thin wedges.

Makes 16 servings.

Tip: Provolone, fontina or mozzarella are good cheeses to use.

Pesto Appetizer Torta

A great make-ahead appetizer using Spinach Pesto Sauce (page 165).

Cream 1 pkg (125 g) light cream cheese and ½ cup (125 mL) butter or margarine until smooth. Alternately layer ⅓ cream cheese mixture and ½ Spinach Pesto Sauce in a plastic-lined bowl, beginning and ending with cheese. Cover and refrigerate until firm. Unmould, remove plastic and serve at room temperature with crackers. Makes several small moulds or 1 large one.

Breakfast

Breakfast-on-the-Run Shakes

How often are you too rushed to make, let alone eat, a sit-down breakfast? One of these breakfast drinks fits the bill on those mornings. But don't limit yourself—these shakes are delicious and refreshing any time of the day.

Peach and Banana Shake

⅓ cup	Spiced Wine Peach Jam (page 30)	75 mL
1	peeled and frozen banana, cut into chunks	1
⅓ cup	vanilla low-fat yogurt	75 mL
½ tsp	vanilla extract	2 mL

Place jam, banana, yogurt and extract in a blender or food processor. Process until smooth. Pour into a glass and enjoy.

Makes about 1 cup (250 mL).

Tip: Replace banana with ¾ cup (175 mL) sliced strawberries, peaches or nectarines.

Tri-Fruit Smoothie

½ cup	sliced mango	125 mL
½ cup	sliced peaches, fresh or frozen	125 mL
⅓ cup	Elegant Oven Strawberry Jam (page 20)	75 mL
⅓ cup	orange juice	75 mL
¼ tsp	almond extract	1 mL

Place mango, peaches, jam, orange juice and extract in a blender or food processor. Process until smooth. Pour into a glass.

Makes about 1 cup (250 mL).

Breakfast Orange Shake

¼ cup	marmalade (preferably an orange-flavoured one from Chapter 3)	50 mL
¼ cup	grapefruit juice	50 mL
¾ cup	milk	175 mL

Place marmalade, juice and milk in a blender or food processor. Process until smooth. Pour into a glass.

Makes 1¼ cups (300 mL).

Apricot Papaya Smoothie

¼ cup	Fresh Apricot Jam (page 28)	50 mL
½	papaya, peeled and cut into chunks	½
½ cup	pineapple juice	125 mL
1 tbsp	lime juice	15 mL

Place jam, papaya, pineapple and lime juice in a blender or food processor. Process until smooth. Pour into a glass.

Makes 1 cup (250 mL).

Pancake and Waffle Sauces

Use one of the flavourful jams or marmalades in Chapters 1 and 3 for an easy-to-make sauce for pouring over waffles, pancakes, French toast or pound cake. We show recipes for 2 but any of the other sweet spreads matched with your choice of fruit juice can be used. Serve them warm for best flavour.

Marmalade Sauce

3 cups	orange juice	750 mL
⅔ cup	marmalade (from Chapter 3)	150 mL
2 tbsp	light brown sugar	25 mL
1 tbsp	each: cornstarch and water	15 mL
1 tsp	butter or margarine	5 mL
1 tsp	rum or vanilla extract	5 mL

1. Bring orange juice to a boil on high heat in a medium saucepan. Reduce heat to medium and boil gently for 15 minutes or until reduced by half. Whisk in marmalade and brown sugar until smooth.
2. Mix cornstarch and water, stir into orange juice mixture. Cook until smooth and slightly thickened. Remove from heat and stir in butter and extract.

Makes about 2½ cups (625 mL).

Mango Blueberry Sauce

1¼ cups	cranberry juice	300 mL
½ cup	orange juice	125 mL
½ cup	Mango Blueberry Freezer Jam (page 38)	125 mL
2 tbsp	granulated sugar	25 mL
1 tbsp	each: cornstarch and water	15 mL
2 tsp	butter or margarine	10 mL
¼ tsp	each: ground cinnamon, nutmeg and ginger	1 mL

1. Bring cranberry juice and orange juice to a boil on high heat in a medium saucepan. Reduce heat to medium and boil gently, uncovered, for 15 minutes or until reduced by half. Whisk in jam and sugar.
2. Mix cornstarch and water, stir into cranberry juice mixture. Cook until smooth and slightly thickened. Remove from heat and stir in spices.

Makes about 1½ cups (375 mL).

Muffins

A batch of muffins in the freezer is always ready to defrost for a quick breakfast or when a friend drops in for coffee or tea.

Bran Ginger Muffins

There is plenty of fibre and flavour in these muffins with their hint of ginger. Using one of the fruit butters (pages 75–77) makes them much lower in fat.

1¼ cups	natural wheat bran or oat bran	300 mL
1 cup	all-purpose flour	250 mL
1 cup	whole wheat flour	250 mL
⅔ cup	lightly packed brown sugar	150 mL
1 tsp	each: baking powder and baking soda	5 mL
¼ tsp	salt	1 mL
1½ cups	buttermilk	375 mL
½ cup	fruit butter (pages 75–77)	125 mL
2 tbsp	vegetable oil	25 mL
2	egg whites	2
3 tbsp	finely chopped crystallized ginger (page 196)	45 mL

1. Combine bran, flours, sugar, baking powder, baking soda and salt in a large mixing bowl.
2. Stir together buttermilk, fruit butter, oil and egg whites in a second bowl. Pour into dry ingredients; stir just until moistened. Stir in ginger.
3. Fill 18 medium non-stick or paper-lined muffin cups with batter, using ½ cup (125 mL) measure. Bake in a 400°F (200°C) oven for 15 minutes or until muffins are lightly browned and firm to the touch.

Makes 18 medium muffins.

Variations:

Apple Ginger Bran Muffin
Add 1 large apple, peeled and chopped.

Raspberry Bran Muffin
Add ¼ cup (50 mL) fresh or frozen raspberries.

Marmalade Fruit Muffins

Marmalade adds moisture and lively flavour to these elegant muffins. Any marmalade can be used, but we like the more intense flavour of those made with Seville oranges.

2 cups	all-purpose flour	500 mL
2 tsp	baking powder	10 mL
½ tsp	salt	2 mL
¼ tsp	baking soda	1 mL
¾ cup	granulated sugar	175 mL
¼ cup	soft butter or margarine	50 mL
2	eggs	2
1 cup	Scotch Seville Marmalade (page 55)	250 mL
¼ cup	orange juice	50 mL
½ cup	dried cranberries, raisins or nuts	125 mL

1. Combine flour, baking powder, salt and baking soda in a medium bowl. Set aside.
2. Cream sugar and butter with an electric mixer or by hand; beat in eggs. Stir in marmalade until blended. Fold in half of flour mixture. Add orange juice, mixing just until combined, and then fold in remaining flour and cranberries.
3. Spoon into greased or paper-lined muffin pans, using ½ cup (125 mL) measure. Bake in a 375°F (190°C) oven for 20 minutes or until lightly browned and firm to the touch.

Makes 18 medium muffins.

Sauces and Marinades for Meat, Fish and Poultry

Sauces

Many of the condiments in Chapters 6 through 10 can be transformed into wonderful sauces for meats, poultry and fish just by adding a few ingredients.

Raspberry Mint Sauce

Serve this colourful and flavourful sauce with roast lamb.

Combine ½ cup (125 mL) Red Wine Raspberry Vinegar (page 181), ¼ cup (50 mL) granulated sugar, 1 tbsp (15 mL) finely chopped fresh mint and freshly ground pepper, to taste. Makes about ⅔ cup (150 mL).

Citrus Dijonnais Sauce

Spread this fruity mustard on fish fillets before cooking in the microwave. It also makes a lively topping for fresh asparagus or green beans.

Combine ¼ cup (50 mL) Dijon-Style Mustard (page 166), 1 tbsp (15 mL) mayonnaise, 1 tsp (5 mL) lemon, orange or lime juice, ½ tsp (2 mL) honey, ¼ tsp (1 mL) each: chopped fresh thyme and grated lemon or orange rind. Makes ⅓ cup (75 mL).

Fruit Coulis

A marvellous sauce to accompany grilled or roasted chicken, veal or pork.

In a blender or food processor, place 6 peeled and chopped fresh apricots or small peaches, ½ cup (125 mL) champagne and ¼ cup (50 mL) Champagne Vinegar (page 180). Process until smooth. Pour purée into a small saucepan and boil gently, uncovered, until reduced to a sauce-like consistency. Stir in 2 tbsp (25 mL) chopped fresh basil or 2 tsp (10 mL) dried. Remove from heat, cool slightly before pouring into a tightly sealed container. Store in the refrigerator for up to 2 weeks. Makes 1 cup (250 mL).

Dijon Cream Sauce for Salmon

A dollop of this sauce also enlivens baked potatoes.

Stir together ½ cup (125 mL) sour cream, 2 tsp (10 mL) Dijon-Style Mustard (page 166) and 1 tbsp (15 mL) chopped fresh dill. Place 4 salmon fillets, skin side down, on a baking tray lined with foil. Lightly brush the top of the fillets with oil. Bake in a 450°F (230°C) oven for 10 minutes or until done. (The skin should stick to the foil.) Spoon a dollop of sauce on salmon and garnish with a sprig of fresh dill. Makes 4 servings.

Raspberry Mustard Coating for Chicken

Raspberry Mustard transforms chicken breasts into an easy festive meal.

Wipe 6 large boneless, skinless chicken breasts with paper towel. Coat with ½ cup (125 mL) Raspberry Mustard Sauce (page 167). Combine ¾ cup (175 mL) dried bread crumbs, 1 tbsp (15 mL) chopped fresh rosemary or 1 tsp (5 mL) dried, a pinch of garlic powder and freshly ground pepper in a shallow bowl. Dredge chicken in bread mixture to coat thoroughly. Bake in a 350°F (180°C) oven for 25 minutes or until juices run clear and chicken is no longer pink inside. Makes 6 servings.

Southwest Corn Sauce

The flavours of southwest cuisine predominate in this unusual marinade. Use it for firm fish such as tuna or swordfish, or for chicken breasts.

Combine 1 cup (250 mL) Fiesta Corn Relish (page 117), ¼ cup (50 mL) canola oil, 2 tbsp (25 mL) each: tomato sauce and finely chopped cilantro in a blender or food processor. Process until smooth. Makes 1½ cups (375 mL).

Marinades for Grilling

Marinades are a great way to add flavour and interest to grilled meats, poultry and fish. Made ahead, they will keep in the refrigerator up to 2 days. When ready to use, place meat or fish in a resealable plastic bag. Pour marinade over, seal bag, turn to coat and refrigerate for 2 hours or overnight (depending on the meat being used and the depth of flavour desired). All foods must be refrigerated while they are marinating. When you remove them from the marinade, pour it into a small saucepan. Bring to a boil, reduce heat and boil gently for 5 minutes; keep warm. Use to baste meat either on the grill or in the oven. Be sure to discard any leftover marinade that has been used.

Citrus Mustard Marinade

Marinate chicken breasts up to 4 hours in the refrigerator before grilling. This marinade is also great to brush on pork chops as they grill.

Combine ½ cup (125 mL) orange juice, ¼ cup (50 mL) each: lemon juice and vegetable oil, 1 tsp (5 mL) each: Dijon-Style Mustard (page 166), dried oregano and Worcestershire sauce, 2 cloves garlic, minced, and a small amount of freshly ground black pepper. Makes 1 cup (250 mL).

Szechwan Marinade

Use this spicy marinade when grilling chicken or shrimp, or when cooking them in a wok or skillet.

Combine ¼ cup (50 mL) tahini (sesame) paste, ¼ cup (50 mL) Five-Pepper Oil (page 178), 3 cloves garlic, minced, and 1 tbsp (15 mL) sherry. Makes ½ cup (125 mL).

Herbes de Provençe Marinade

A light marinade, it is perfect for fillets of fish such as orange roughy, white fish or tuna.
Combine ¼ cup (50 mL) each: white wine and olive oil, 2 tbsp (25 mL) each:
Provençe-Style Vinegar (page 181) and fresh lemon juice, 1 clove garlic, minced,
and 1 sprig fresh rosemary, minced. Makes ¾ cup (175 mL).

Asian Whisky Marinade

Use this marinade on lean lamb, chicken or fish.
Whisk together ½ cup (125 mL) Asian Whisky Sauce (page 170), 2 tbsp (25 mL)
each: lemon juice, ketchup and 1 clove garlic, minced. Makes ¾ cup (175 mL).

Oriental Plum Sauce Marinade

Brush Hoisin-Style Plum Sauce directly on meat or poultry as it grills. These few additions
make it even better.
Combine 1 cup (250 mL) Hoisin-Style Plum Sauce (page 40), ¼ cup (50 mL)
finely chopped fresh cilantro, 2 tbsp (25 mL) dry sherry, 1 tsp (5 mL) sesame oil
and 2 cloves garlic, minced. Makes 1 cup (250 mL).

Apricot Marinade

This is a wonderful glaze for spare ribs, as well as a good marinade for Cornish hens, pork chops
or whole pork tenderloin. Marinate pork for 8 hours or longer and chicken for 3 to 4 hours.
Combine ½ cup (125 mL) dry white wine, ¼ cup (50 mL) each: Fresh Apricot
Jam (page 28) or Microwave Brandied Apricot Jam (page 40), vegetable oil and
white wine vinegar, 1 tbsp (15 mL) Dijon-Style Mustard (page 166) and 1 tsp
(5 mL) soy sauce. Makes about 1¼ cups (300 mL).

Basil Lemon Marinade

Brush on chicken pieces as they cook on the barbecue.
Combine ¼ cup (50 mL) Basil Oil with Lemon and Black Peppercorns (page 176),
2 tbsp (25 mL) each: lemon juice, balsamic vinegar and finely chopped onion,
1 tsp (5 mL) freshly ground black pepper, ½ tsp (2 mL) dried thyme and 1 garlic
clove, minced. Makes ½ cup (125 mL).

Oriental Marinade

Marinate beef and pork in Oriental Marinade, then brush it on during grilling to add inter-
esting flavours. Refrigerate any leftovers to cube and toss with salad greens or mesclun.
Combine ¼ cup (50 mL) rice wine vinegar, 3 tbsp (45 mL) Nut-Infused Oil (page
179), 2 tbsp (25 mL) pineapple juice, 1 tbsp (15 mL) soy sauce, ½ tsp (2 mL) each:
granulated sugar and minced gingerroot and ⅛ tsp (0.5 mL) each: salt and freshly
ground pepper. Makes about ½ cup (125 mL).

Raspberry Orange Marinade

Raspberry Orange Vinaigrette (page 184) is a perfect marinade for grilled chicken and pork.

Vegetables

Mustard Butters for Vegetables

Keep these versatile butters on hand in the refrigerator to serve with such vegetables as asparagus, green beans, cauliflower and broccoli. We also like them with grilled chicken and fish.

Dijon Mustard Butter
Combine 1 large clove garlic, minced, 1 tsp (5 mL) drained capers, rinsed, and ⅛ tsp (0.5 mL) each: salt and freshly ground pepper in a small bowl. Stir in ½ cup (125 mL) softened butter, ¼ cup (50 mL) Dijon-Style Mustard (page 166) and 3 tbsp (45 mL) chopped fresh basil or 1 tbsp (15 mL) dried. Place in a small covered container and refrigerate until needed. Makes about ¾ cup (175 mL).

Marmalade Mustard Butters
Combine ⅓ cup (75 mL) marmalade (pages 53–66) with 2 tbsp (25 mL) Dijon-Style Mustard (page 166) and 1 tbsp (15 mL) lemon or orange juice in a small saucepan. Heat until marmalade is melted and mixture hot. Drizzle over cooked vegetables. Makes about ½ cup (125 mL).

Sun-Dried Tomato Mustard Butter
Combine ¼ cup (50 mL) Sun-Dried Tomato Mustard (page 168), 1 tbsp (15 mL) each: orange juice and honey. Makes ⅓ cup (75 mL).

Potato Bake with Relish

Relish transforms an ordinary potato into an out-of-the-ordinary supper dish. Made quickly in the microwave, it can be ready in short order. Try it with Barbecue Relish (page 115) or Processor Apple Mint Relish (page 122). And for an entrée, layer slices of cooked chicken, ham or salami with the vegetables.

1 tbsp	olive oil	15 mL
1	onion, thinly sliced	1
1	small green pepper, chopped	1
2	cloves garlic, minced	2
½ cup	Barbecue or Processor Apple Mint Relish	125 mL
5 cups	thinly sliced potatoes (about 2 lb/1 kg)	1.25 L
1 cup	grated Parmesan cheese	250 mL

1. Heat oil in a large non-stick skillet; cook onion, green pepper and garlic on medium high until tender, about 3 minutes. Remove from heat and stir in relish.
2. Arrange ⅓ of potatoes in an 8-cup (2-L) casserole. Cover with half the vegetables. Sprinkle with ⅓ of cheese. Repeat layers and top with remaining potatoes. Cover and microwave at High (100%) for 10 minutes. Sprinkle with remaining cheese, reduce power to Medium (70%) and microwave for 5 minutes. Let stand for 5 minutes before serving.

Makes 4 servings.

Provençe-Style Grilled Vegetables

An example of how very easy it is to make a zippy marinade from one of our specialty vinegars.

¼ cup	Provençe-style Vinegar (page 181)	50 mL
2 tbsp	liquid honey	25 mL
1 tbsp	canola oil	15 mL
½ tsp	each: freshly ground pepper and salt	2 mL
4	cloves garlic, minced	4
4	plum tomatoes, halved	4
2	zucchini, cut lengthwise into ¼-inch (6-mm) slices	2
1	medium eggplant, cut crosswise into 1-inch (2.5-cm) thick slices	1
1	sweet red pepper, seeded and cut into 8 wedges	1
1	Vidalia or Spanish onion, cut into 2-inch (5-cm) thick wedges	1
1	small bunch kale, coarsely chopped	1

1. Combine vinegar, honey, oil, pepper, salt and garlic in a small bowl.
2. Combine tomatoes, zucchini, eggplant, red pepper, onion and kale. Divide vegetables and vinegar mixture between 2 large resealable plastic bags. Seal bags and refrigerate for up to 1 hour; turn bags occasionally.
3. Preheat grill to medium high and spray rack with non-stick coating. Place vegetables on rack; reserve marinade. Grill about 7 minutes on each side or until onion is tender, basting with reserved marinade.

Makes 8 servings.

Tip: Kale becomes quite crisp during grilling, and is very tasty.

Vegetable Stir-Fry with Oregano Pepper Vinaigrette

Using one of the recipes for vinaigrettes is a great way to add that extra-special flavour boost to any stir-fry.

1 tbsp	canola oil	15 mL
¾ cup	chopped green onions	175 mL
1 cup	diagonally sliced carrot	250 mL
1 cup	sliced yellow sweet pepper	250 mL
1 cup	sliced green or red sweet pepper	250 mL
3 cups	broccoli florets	750 mL
1 cup	fresh bean sprouts	250 mL
¼ cup	Oregano Pepper Vinaigrette (page 184)	50 mL

Heat oil in a large non-stick skillet or wok over medium-high heat. Add onions and stir-fry for 1 minute. Add carrot and peppers; stir-fry for 1 minute. Add broccoli; cover and cook for 2 minutes. Add sprouts and vinaigrette. Bring to a boil, uncovered, and cook for about 30 seconds, stirring constantly.

Makes 4 to 6 servings.

Salads and Sandwiches

Salads

Salsas and relishes give marvellous eye appeal and taste to potato and pasta salads. The moisture they add allows us to use less oil in the dressings. See page 183 for vinaigrettes for tossed green salads.

Potato Salsa Salad

4	large potatoes, halved	4
½ cup	each: chopped seedless cucumber and green pepper	125 mL
1	green onion, sliced	1
½ cup	Gazpacho Salsa (page 128)	125 mL
1 tbsp	each: olive oil and red wine vinegar	15 mL
2 tbsp	chopped fresh cilantro	25 mL
	Red leaf lettuce	

1. Boil potatoes until tender; drain and cool until easy to handle. Peel, cube and place in a large bowl. When potatoes are cool, stir in cucumber, green pepper and onion.
2. Combine salsa, oil, vinegar and cilantro. Pour over potatoes and stir. Cover and chill until ready to serve.

Makes 4–6 servings.

Garden Pasta Salad

1	pkg (12 oz/375 g) fusilli, small shell or other pasta	1
1½ cups	relish (see Tip)	375 mL
½ cup	each: plain yogurt and mayonnaise	125 mL
1 tsp	each: garlic powder and basil leaves	5 mL
1	sweet red or green pepper, chopped	1
1 cup	frozen green peas, thawed	250 mL
½ cup	chopped green onion	125 mL
	Freshly ground pepper	

1. Cook pasta in a large amount of boiling salted water according to manufacturer's directions or until al dente. Drain, rinse in cold water and drain thoroughly. Set aside.

2. Combine relish, yogurt, mayonnaise, garlic powder and basil in a large bowl. Stir in pasta, red pepper, peas and onion. Sprinkle with black pepper, cover and refrigerate for several hours.

Makes 8 generous servings.

> Tip: We like to use Fiesta Corn Relish, Processor Apple Mint Relish or Easy Oven Relish (pages 117, 114 and 122).

Zucchini Corn Salad

This tasty summer salad needs little preparation time.

Combine 2 tbsp (25 mL) oil, 1 tbsp (15 mL) wine or other vinegar, ½ tsp (2 mL) granulated sugar, ¼ tsp (1 mL) salt and ½ cup (125 mL) Fiesta Corn Relish in a medium bowl. Stir in 1½ cups (375 mL) diced zucchini and 1 small chopped tomato. Cover and refrigerate for 2 hours or more before serving. Makes 2 cups (500 mL).

Sandwich Spreads

Ideal for canapés or sandwiches, these interesting spreads "open the lid" on our chutney and salsa recipes.

Crab Spread with Chutney

1	can (6 oz/170 g) crab meat	1
3	marinated artichoke pieces, chopped	3
1 cup	tightly packed spinach leaves, chopped	250 mL
1	green onion, chopped	1
2 tbsp	chopped almonds	25 mL
⅓ cup	fruit chutney (see Tip)	75 mL
2 tbsp	light mayonnaise	25 mL
1 tbsp	lemon juice	15 mL
⅛ tsp	salt, pepper and curry powder, optional	0.5 mL

1. Flake crab meat and combine with artichoke, spinach, onion and almonds.
2. Stir together chutney, mayonnaise and lemon juice. Stir into crab mixture. Refrigerate for several hours for flavours to blend. Taste and adjust seasonings with a pinch of salt, pepper and curry powder, if desired.

Makes 2 cups (500 mL).

> Tip: We like Mango Papaya Chutney (page 145) or Red Pepper Apricot Chutney (page 150).

Sweet Treats

Coffee Cake with Cranberry Conserve

Brandied Cranberry Conserve (page 72) adds a festive note and bright flavour to coffee cake. Try other jams and marmalades with coffee cake, too.

Streusel Topping

½ cup	lightly packed brown sugar	125 mL
¼ cup	all-purpose flour	50 mL
¼ cup	soft butter or margarine	50 mL

Cake

¾ cup	granulated sugar	175 mL
¼ cup	soft shortening	50 mL
1	egg	1
½ cup	milk	125 mL
1⅓ cups	all-purpose flour	325 mL
2 tsp	baking powder	10 mL
½ tsp	salt	2 mL
1 cup	Brandied Cranberry Conserve (page 72)	250 mL

To Make Topping:

Combine sugar, flour and butter in a food processor. Process with on/off turns until fine crumbs occur. Set aside.

To Make Cake:

1. Cream sugar, shortening and egg until smooth with an electric mixer or by hand; beat in milk.
2. Combine flour, baking powder and salt; stir into egg mixture. Spread batter into a greased 8-inch (2-L) square baking dish. Top with spoonfuls of conserve and sprinkle with topping. Bake in a 375°F (190°C) oven for 35 minutes or until a toothpick inserted in centre comes out clean. Serve warm.

Makes 9 servings.

Light Chocolate Brownies

These fat-free chocolate brownies taste like the real thing. They use Baker's Prune Butter (page 76) as a fat substitute. Its density and moisture give a taste and mouth-feel very much like brownies made with butter or margarine. The dark colour of the prune butter makes it especially appropriate for making dark-coloured cakes like brownies.

1 cup	cake and pastry flour	250 mL
¾ cup	granulated sugar	175 mL
½ cup	unsweetened cocoa	125 mL
1 tsp	baking powder	5 mL
½ tsp	salt	2 mL
⅓ cup	corn syrup	75 mL
⅓ cup	Baker's Prune Butter (page 76)	75 mL
2	beaten egg whites	2
	Icing sugar, optional	

1. Stir together flour, sugar, cocoa, baking powder and salt in a large bowl.
2. Stir in syrup, prune butter and egg whites. Spoon batter into a lightly greased 8-inch (2-L) square baking pan. Bake in a 350°F (180°C) oven for 30 minutes or until top springs back when lightly touched. Cook completely on a wire rack before cutting into 16 squares. Sprinkle lightly with icing sugar, if desired.

Makes 16 squares.

Tip: After the squares are cool, they keep fresh for longer by being frozen in a tightly sealed container.

Spiced Fig Jam Bars

Australian Spiced Dried Fig Jam makes a marvellous rich cookie filling. Try it in these quick-to-make bars. Other fruity jams such as Spiced Wine Peach, Winter Apricot Pineapple and Sour Cherry Gooseberry (pages 30, 34 and 24) are delicious variations.

¾ cup	granulated sugar	175 mL
½ cup	butter or margarine	125 mL
2	eggs	2
1 tsp	vanilla extract	5 mL
2½ cups	all-purpose flour	625 mL
½ tsp	salt	2 mL
¼ tsp	baking soda	1 mL
1½ cups	Australian Spiced Dried Fig Jam (page 33)	375 mL

1. Cream sugar, butter, eggs and vanilla with an electric mixer or by hand in a large mixing bowl until smooth.
2. Combine flour, salt and baking soda; stir into butter mixture, forming a soft dough.
3. Divide dough into 2 parts. Roll half of dough on a floured surface into an 8- x 12-inch (20- x 30-cm) rectangle. Spread half of jam along the centre of dough, leaving approximately a 2-inch (5-cm) strip on each side. Using a flat lifter, fold sides of dough to cover jam. Cut into 4 crosswise sections and place on a baking sheet. Repeat with second half of dough.
4. Bake in a 400°F (200°C) oven for 12 minutes or until slightly browned on edges. Transfer to a cooling rack. When cool, cut each into 2 lengthwise pieces, then cut each piece into 3 bars.

Makes 48 bars.

Tip: For special occasions, cut dough into 2-inch (5-cm) diameter rounds, spread half with a bit of jam, fold other half over to cover filling and seal edges with a fork.

Index